D0498645

FOLLOWING CHRIST

FOLLOWING CHRIST

*The Parable of the Divers
and More Good News*

Stephen E. Robinson

Deseret Book Company
Salt Lake City, Utah

To the many humble followers of Christ in
the old La Cañada Ward (1950–64) who counseled,
led, and taught; who drove, coached, and cooked;
and who gave their time, their food, their homes,
and quite often their love; and especially to
Maude Barron and Cy Watson of blessed memory

Library of Congress Cataloging-in-Publication Data

Following Christ : the parable of the divers and more good news /
Stephen E. Robinson.
  p. cm.
Includes bibliographical references and index.
ISBN 1-57345-059-6 (hardback)
  1. Spiritual life—Mormon Church. 2. Jesus Christ—Mormon
interpretations. 3. Mormon Church—Doctrines. I. Title.
BX8656.R64   1995
248.4'89332—dc20   95-683
                                          CIP

Printed in the United States of America

10 9 8 7 6 5 4 3 2 1

CONTENTS

Preface   vii

Acknowledgments   ix

1 Getting to the Kingdom   1

2 Enduring to the End   21

3 The Fall of Adam and Eve   43

4 Faith and Works   65

5 Hazards to Endurance   91

6 The Prime Directive   129

Index   161

PREFACE

Some time ago I wrote a book about first principles of the gospel that some members of the Church have found helpful. That book, *Believing Christ: The Parable of the Bicycle and Other Good News,* describes what it means to have faith in the Lord Jesus Christ and to be justified by faith in him through the gospel covenant, the fullness of which has been restored in these latter days. However, as many readers have pointed out, our lives do not end once we enter the covenant. Having been born again, we are then faced with the anticlimactic necessity of *living* again. Perhaps the greatest spiritual frustration many people encounter is that without exception we mortals are *converted* long before we can be *perfected.* That means all of us must limp along for a considerable period of time in which our commitment and desire are not matched by our actual performance, and in which we must simply trust God to take care of us—warts and all. That condition is not limited to the spiritually inept but is the common lot of everyone in the Church. So the next logical question is, "If God doesn't require me to be absolutely perfect immediately upon conversion, what *does* he expect of me, and how am I supposed to come up with it? Now that I've been born again, what do I *do* with the rest of my life—and how do I do it?"

One of the scriptural terms most often used for what God expects of the converted is *endurance.* Having entered the covenant of grace at baptism, we are asked to endure in it until the end of our lives. Thus the phrase *enduring to the end* adequately describes our covenant obligation between our conversion and our death.

Where *Believing Christ* dealt with *entering* the covenant, this book will focus on *staying* in the covenant. The former book dealt with believing Christ and coming to Christ; the present volume deals with following and worshipping Christ. If being truly converted is to accept Christ as Lord and to make him the Lord of our lives, then this must somehow be reflected *in* our lives—but how? How does being born again translate into behavior *after* our conversion? After all, faith and works are not the polar opposites some theologians would make them; rather, in the covenant they are yokefellows or two sides of the same coin. It is a little silly to talk endlessly about *coming* to Christ without ever mentioning where we are once we've gotten there. The other side of the coin—the role of works in the gospel of Christ—is the subject of this book.

ACKNOWLEDGMENTS

I would like to thank those who have made it possible for me to write this book: My Sunday School class for drawing much of it out of me. Fawn and Carol Morgan for giving me a place to hide out and write. George Karlsven for helping to keep me alive by marching me around the Grandview Hill for exercise. Debbie Parker, Sue Ostler, Larry Dahl, Dennis Largey, and Karen Stoddard for reading the manuscript and offering suggestions. And Deseret Book Company for pursuing the project but with patience when I was distracted by other obligations. I have been blessed with good secretaries—special thanks to Michelle Green and Connie Lankford. And, as always, I acknowledge Janet, my inspiration, whose love blows gently on the dim coals of my abilities and coaxes them for a time to glow slightly brighter.

Chapter One

GETTING TO THE KINGDOM

What must I *do* to get into the kingdom of God? On this point the scriptures are surprisingly clear and explicit. For example, in the Gospel of John, Jesus is recorded to have said, "God so loved the world, that he gave his only begotten Son, that whosoever *believeth* in him should not perish, but have everlasting life" (John 3:16, emphasis added). In Mark's Gospel, as the resurrected Jesus sent his apostles out to preach to the world, he taught them that "he that *believeth* and is *baptized* shall be saved" (Mark 16:16, emphasis added). Consider the following from the Book of Mormon: "The Father commandeth all men, everywhere, to *repent* and *believe* in me. And whoso *believeth* in me, and is *baptized*, the same shall be saved; and they are they who shall inherit the kingdom of God" (3 Nephi 11:32–33, emphasis added). The vital significance of these and many other similar passages of scripture that could be cited on this subject often escapes us. It is this: The critical elements referred to in these scriptures concerning being saved, or receiving everlasting life, or inheriting the kingdom of God are all elements associated not with the distant future or with how we live the rest of our lives; rather, they are things we do to enter the covenant of the gospel. They come at the *beginning* of one's life in Christ and membership in the Church. In other words, to "get right with God" and become heirs of salvation is to come unto Christ and enter the covenant of his gospel. This is done by having faith in Christ, repenting of our sins, and being baptized by immersion for the remission of sins. We then receive from God the wonderful gift of the Holy Ghost. The primary focus is therefore not upon the coming judgment day but rather upon our initial conversion to Christ.

With this perspective in mind, consider these words of Moses in the Pearl of Great Price: "The Lord God called upon men by the Holy Ghost everywhere and commanded them that they should *repent*; and as many as *believed* in the Son, and *repented* of their sins, should be saved; and as many as *believed* not and *repented* not, should be damned; and the words went forth out of the mouth of God in a firm decree; wherefore they must be fulfilled" (Moses 5:14–15; emphasis added). Believing, repenting, being baptized, receiving the Holy Spirit—*clearly*, these are the elements most directly associated in the scriptures with being saved, entering the kingdom, or receiving eternal life. And all of them come at the *beginning* of our life in Christ—not at the end.

Latter-day Saints have hesitated to use the term *being*

saved, as many Protestants do, as an equivalent for "being converted" or "coming to Christ," since we understand that as long as we live, this salvation is *conditional* upon our enduring to the end. Since some Christians would dispute that there is such a condition, it is worth reading the Savior's own words in Matthew 24:13: "But he that shall endure unto the end, the same shall be saved" (see also Matthew 10:22; Mark 13:13; 2 Nephi 31:15). Hence Latter-day Saints hesitate to speak of salvation as a "done deal" in this life (not trusting themselves to remain faithful, I suppose). Latter-day Saints have generally reserved the term *saved* only for our status after the judgment, when that status is an accomplished fact rather than merely a divine promise conditioned on our "enduring." Other Christians prefer to use *saved* for the status conferred upon us at the time we enter the covenant, which is equally proper and scriptural.[1] Either way, it is true that while converted believers remain faithful, they are indeed also "saved" in the present tense, though saved conditionally, according to the Savior himself, upon their enduring to the end (Matthew 10:22, 24:13, etc.).

Consider further Moses 6:59: " . . . even so ye must be born again into the kingdom of heaven, of water, and of the Spirit, and be cleansed by blood, even the blood of

---

[1]Some non-Mormons think this "being saved" is irrevocable; Latter-day Saints would disagree. Others simply assume that the "saved" will just want to remain faithful. LDS differences with the latter are largely semantic rather than theological.

mine Only Begotten; that ye might be sanctified from all sin, and enjoy the words of eternal life in this world, and eternal life in the world to come, even immortal glory." Here again we are instructed that the critical threshold we cross to be "born again into the kingdom of heaven," to be "sanctified," and to enjoy "eternal life" and "glory" is being baptized and receiving the gift of the Holy Ghost—that is, *entering* the gospel covenant. Once these steps have been taken, we become part of Christ. We are part of his metaphorical body, the Church (1 Corinthians 12:27), and we are justified through the grace of Jesus Christ our Savior. In other words, even though we are still personally imperfect, we are declared to be innocent because *he* is innocent and we are *part* of him.

Through faith, repentance, and baptism, we are incorporated into Christ and receive a new joint identity; we are no longer just ourselves—we are now Christ, and he is us—just as a husband and wife become one through the covenant of marriage. Just as a wife normally takes her husband's name and becomes heir to his property, so we take Christ's name upon us and become heirs of his kingdom through his death. Having thus become joined together in one, we become a new, composite creature (2 Corinthians 5:17) composed of a finite part (us) and an infinite part (Christ). Since Christ is infinite, it is *his* character that defines the nature of this new creature and that determines the verdict to be pronounced upon us at the judgment. Therefore, as long as we remain one with Christ in this new joint relationship—in the covenant of the gospel—we are, for the time being, justified and redeemed on account of *his* righteousness (2 Nephi 2:3) because we have become part of him, and his righteousness is therefore ours too. In the gospel partnership, since we are one with Christ, we receive credit for what Christ has done, and it is his infinite merit rather than our own flawed performance that finally secures a "not guilty" verdict for the new creature we have become in and with Christ. This whole process is called "justification by faith in Christ" (D&C 20:30; Galatians 2:16).[2]

Once justified in this manner through our faith in Christ, we are sanctified or made holy by receiving the gift of the Holy Ghost (3 Nephi 27:20; Alma 13:12), and those who have been so sanctified are called *Saints* (from the Latin *sancti* or "holy ones"). The word *sanctified* means "made holy." Having been declared innocent (justification by faith), we are then worthy to receive the Holy Ghost and are made holy (sanctified) by receiving that gift. All members of the Church in good faith have received the gift of the Holy Ghost and been sanctified by receiving it; that is why they are referred to collectively as "the Saints." Thus Paul addresses his first epistle to the Corinthians "to them that are sanctified in Christ Jesus, called to be saints" (1 Corinthians 1:2). Those who have been sanctified or made holy through Christ in these latter days are specifically called "Latter-day Saints."

---

[2]This is the subject of my former book, *Believing Christ*, to which the reader is referred if the treatment here is a little too sketchy.

Thus for us members, even our designation as Saints acknowledges that we have *already* been made holy through the atonement of Christ though we are still in the flesh and are still struggling with mortality.

Strictly speaking, what *we* do to enter the kingdom is to have faith in Jesus Christ, repent, and submit to baptism. What *God* does to show his involvement in the process and to complete the covenant is to give us the Holy Ghost. Thus we emphasize it is the *gift* of the Holy Ghost we receive at confirmation, and this gift is God's token to us that the covenant of baptism we have entered into is accepted by him. If we truly receive the Holy Ghost and enjoy that great gift, it is proof that we are truly in the covenant and in the kingdom from that moment—justified by our faith in Christ and sanctified by the gift of the Holy Ghost.

So the great divide between the saved and the unsaved, between those who inherit the kingdom and those who do not, between those who are right with God and those who are not, isn't just who is "good" and who is "bad," for technically speaking we are *all* bad in some degree (Romans 3:23; Mosiah 2:21). Rather, the great divide is whether we accept or reject the covenant with the Savior Jesus Christ, the only being in eternity who can make us innocent by incorporating us into his infinite, perfect, and sinless self. And this great divide is crossed when we first make the covenant and *enter* the Church of Jesus Christ. Since Christ is already in the kingdom of God, when we come unto *him* we also of necessity come into *it*.

What I want to emphasize in this regard ought to be self evident, but apparently a lot of us miss it. For members of The Church of Jesus Christ of Latter-day Saints, these critical steps, which are equivalent to entering into the kingdom, *are already behind us*. They are history. Therefore we are not waiting to see what some future verdict will decide. If we are in the covenant, the verdict is already in, and so are we. Since having faith, repenting, being baptized, and receiving the Holy Ghost all take place *before* we are counted members of the Church, those who are already members in good faith are already in the kingdom. We are in it *now*. For most of the readers of this book, the glorious threshold has already been crossed, and the doors of the kingdom have already closed gently behind us! If we are truly in his church, then we are truly in his kingdom.[3]

Yet many of the Latter-day Saints who already believe in Christ, have already begun their repentance, have already been baptized, and have already received the gift of the Holy Ghost—in short, have already entered into the covenant—many of these people continue to think and act as though the determination of whether they are in or out of the kingdom; saved or damned; celestial,

---

[3]Of course, this assumes that one is in the Church by informed choice and not merely as a coincidence of birth or for reasons of "bad faith," such as family, social, or economic reasons.

terrestrial, or telestial is somehow still in the future. They have been influenced by the common traditions of the world. Too many of the Saints see their mortal lives in the Church as a kind of porch or anteroom outside the kingdom doors. If they work hard enough in this life, they feel, the doors will eventually open up and admit them at some future time. *Horsefeathers!* Having been handed the good news of salvation, these people decline to open the envelope but continue to twist in the wind, wondering from day to day if they are being "good enough" to qualify for what they in fact *already* possess. They are like defendants in a court case who have been found innocent but who weren't paying attention when the verdict was read and somehow missed it. So hours later they're still sitting alone in the courtroom, wringing their hands and praying for acquittal—long after the judge and the jury have rendered their verdict and gone home.

Those members who think their place in the kingdom is not yet established either did not enter the Church in good faith in the first place or else came to Christ honestly but did not understand what happened when they believed, repented, were baptized, and received the gift of the Holy Ghost—that they passed through the strait and narrow gate and now stand, conditionally, in the kingdom of God. There is more to be done, but we are *through* the gate. The gate was faith, repentance, and baptism: "For the gate by which ye should enter is repentance and baptism by water" (2 Nephi 31:17). As the Lord revealed to Emma Smith through the Prophet Joseph, "All those who receive my gospel *are* sons and daughters in my kingdom" (D&C 25:1, emphasis added). And God cannot lie.

Perhaps one reason so many people miss this is that (as is so often the case) there is an ambiguity here in the way a term is used in scripture. Sometimes, but not always, "the kingdom" or "the kingdom of God" means the *future* kingdom, the physical reality of coming glory. That is the sense, for example, in 1 Corinthians 15:50, 2 Nephi 10:25, Alma 41:4, and D&C 6:13. But in other passages "the kingdom" is a collective noun for the society of the Saints and is therefore usually equivalent with "the Church," as in the phrase "the Church and kingdom of God." This is the meaning, for example, in Luke 11:20, D&C 35:27, and D&C 115:19. In this sense the kingdom isn't real estate, but it is here among us nevertheless (see Luke 17:21 where "within" should be translated "among"). The Doctrine and Covenants makes a useful distinction in section 65:6 between "the kingdom of God" (the present kingdom of which we are members through baptism) and "the kingdom of heaven" (the future political kingdom to be established in glory). However, these are not two different kingdoms but rather two aspects of the same kingdom. Further, this special distinction in terms can't be pressed too far, for it is not always observed in scripture.[4]

---

[4]For example, it doesn't work at Alma 9:25 or 1 Corinthians 15:50. Moreover, the Gospel of Matthew uses the term *kingdom of heaven* where Luke and Mark have *kingdom of God*. This usage is not intended to specify the future kingdom as opposed to the present one;

I like the distinction made by the Topical Guide in listing the references to "kingdom" under two headings, "Kingdom of God, in Heaven" and "Kingdom of God, on Earth." This recognizes both the present and future aspects of the one, single "Kingdom of God." On the one hand, the kingdom is present here and now as the Church and as the fellowship of the Saints. On the other hand, as a political and geographical reality it must wait until the second coming of our Lord.

Just as the kingdom is here in one sense but in one sense not yet here, so on the one hand (since God's promise is sure and certain), my place in the coming kingdom is sure and certain (unless I choose to leave), but on the other hand, my glorification hasn't actually happened yet. Though I am already redeemed from the Fall through Christ, I must still suffer the effects of the Fall in this life. So in one sense I am already redeemed or "saved"—the atonement has been completed and the victory is won—but in another sense I am not completely saved *yet*, since I still struggle with mortality, will surely die, and will not be actually glorified until later. Understood as the society of those who *are going to receive* celestial glory (if they are true and faithful), the kingdom is here now, and we are "saved" now; understood as the society of those who

---

rather Matthew, as a thoroughly Jewish document, seeks reverently to avoid the too-frequent repetition of the noun *God* by substituting the noun *heaven*.

have received celestial glory, the kingdom is obviously still in the future.

I doubt that Latter-day Saints ever will, or even should, adopt Protestant terminology and begin regularly talking about "being saved" in the present tense. There is a risk that other Protestant interpretations might come along with their terminology. Nevertheless, we *must* understand that conditional salvation is a present real-ity—that we can be certain *now* of what God has promised for the future. After all, Latter-day Saints appro-priately talk about "being sealed" in the present tense even though we know these sealings are conditioned on our faithfulness and will not be fully actualized until later. I suggest that *being saved* can be similarly under-stood. We are "saved" now in the same way that most of us are "sealed" now—on condition of continued faithful-ness. And assuming that we will be faithful, we can refer to ourselves as "saved" even though the full actualization of this promise will not occur until the resurrection, just as we commonly refer to ourselves as "sealed" in the same way.[5]

Perhaps I can illustrate the ambiguous already-here-but-not-yet-here nature of the kingdom or of "being

---

[5]Brigham Young had no trouble with using the word *saved* in terms of the present: "Our work is a work of the present. The salvation we are seeking is for the present, and, sought correctly, it can be obtained, and be continually enjoyed. If it continues today, it is upon the same principle that it will continue tomorrow, the next day, the next week, or the next year, and, we might say, the next eternity" (*Journal of Discourses* 1:131).

saved" with an example. I recently took my young daughter, Mary, fishing, and it was important to me that she catch a fish. So I cast the line in for her, and when I felt a bite, I solidly set the hook. Then I stripped some line off the reel and handed the pole to Mary. I waited a few seconds, then suggested that she reel in slowly. After a few turns of the handle she felt the fish tugging on her line, and shrieking with delight she hauled it to the bank.

Now, my question is this: At what point in time was the fish actually caught? Did I catch it when I set the hook and made the outcome sure and certain, or did Mary catch it when she physically pulled the fish out onto the bank? A case can rightly be made either way. Similarly, when do we inherit the kingdom—when are we "saved"? Is it when the hook is set—that is, when the determinative events have taken place that make the final outcome certain on the single condition of endurance (the atonement of Christ and my entering the covenant), or is it when we actually rise in celestial glory and receive what was so certainly promised? A case can rightly be made either way.

The bottom line is that for those of us who have come to Christ, the hook is set, and God intends to reel us in. So, unless we wilfully cut the line, we may properly anticipate with joy the coming of what is promised. We are members *now* of a kingdom that is coming, and unless we choose to commit spiritual suicide, we are entitled to consider ourselves saved. I suspect that properly understanding this great truth would help many of

the Latter-day Saints more readily feel the "joy," "rejoicing," "confidence," and "hope" the good news of the
gospel is supposed to bring.

Several years ago some friends of mine adopted an
older child from the Third World who had lived a very
difficult life before coming to the United States. For a
long time their greatest frustration in dealing with their
new daughter was her crippling insecurity: she couldn't
believe she was safe. She paid slavish, obsessive attention
to every word her new parents uttered for fear she would
make a mistake and be sent back "there" because of it.
She was so terrified of what her parents might do if she
weren't "good," if she weren't *perfect,* that she could not
for a long time enter into the relationship of love and
trust they desired to have with her. They couldn't make
suggestions for her improvement, or constructively criti-
cize, or show any kind of irritation or impatience with
her whatever without sending the poor girl into a panic,
tearfully begging for forgiveness and for "just one more
chance." It was heart-wrenching to see. Over and over
they tried to reassure her that she could have all the
"chances" she needed; that their decision to adopt her
was eternal, irrevocable, and no longer open to reevalua-
tion; that she was part of their family now and need not
fear she would ever be sent away. "Please trust us," they
would plead. "Don't you know that only *you* can break
the bond that now holds us together? It will never be severed on our side. Your place with us is secure. As long as
you want to stay, this is your home." Still, it took years

for her to fully realize that she wasn't being evaluated for possible deportation every time she made a mistake.

Well, spiritually some of us are just like her. We've been so traumatized by our experiences in the world that we have a hard time accepting the love of God and believing we could possibly have a place in his family. *Already* recipients of his love and *already* adopted his sons and daughters, some of us are still trying to earn his affection and get into the family. Our inability to accept his merciful gifts and tender mercies gets in the way of the better relationship we might have with God if we only knew our proper place in his love and in his kingdom and then progressed from there.

I wonder if those of us who have been reborn sons and daughters of God through the atonement of Christ don't frustrate our Heavenly Father when we panic at our every mistake for fear he will stop loving us and send us back to the world. I can almost hear him entreating us, "Please trust me. Don't you know that only *you* can break the bond that now holds us together? It will never be severed on my side. Your place with me is secure. As long as you want to stay, this is your home." Again, we need to believe what the Lord told Emma Smith: "All those who receive my gospel are sons and daughters in my kingdom (D&C 25:1)." And it must be so, for God cannot lie.

As we raise our own children, we don't say, "That was a real good job, young man. If you keep that up, you just might earn yourself a place in this family! Conceivably (now don't get your hopes too high, boy), you could even

become our son." No, that's not how we do it. First the
family relationship is created, and then that relationship
becomes the basis for subsequent training. Without such
a relationship, we have no right to impose any training
upon or expect any obedience from anyone. I suspect it is
no different with God. When we come to Christ with bro-
ken hearts and contrite spirits, he encircles us in the arms
of his love (2 Nephi 1:15) and adopts us as his sons and
daughters. Then, as a loving parent, he teaches us how to
become what he is. But the bond, the relationship entered
into by our own desire, precedes the training and is what
justifies the training and discipline he gives us and makes
it bearable.

Relative to the kingdom of God, most people are "out
until they're in." That is, they are not members of the
kingdom until they accept the gospel and enter into the
covenant relationship. But in stark contrast to this, the
members of the Church are "in until they're out." That
is, all who are in the covenant are God's children now,
and they will remain in the kingdom until they choose to
leave. And if we accept his training and his discipline—if
we endure to the end—we will *still* be his children at the
great day.[6]

Perhaps the best analogy is that favorite of the scriptures: Christ as the bridegroom, the Church as the bride,
and the gospel covenant as a marriage. When, then, is this

---

[6]Obviously, I am referring here to being born again as children of
Christ rather than to our premortal spirit birth.

marriage performed? When do we and the Savior become one by covenant? Not at some future judgment, but at baptism! We're not just living together; we are in the Church, and the Church is the bride, so it must follow that we enjoy the marriage relationship *now*. Having been joined to the bridegroom by the gospel covenant, we cannot go through life like common-law partners, hoping that someday he will marry us and make the arrangement legitimate. We're *already* married—and he expects us to know it and to act like it!

Now it is true that *we* can decide we no longer want to stay in the covenant and in the kingdom. We can rebel against God, violate our agreement with him, and exercise our option to leave. We can file for divorce from Christ. But that decision is not up to God; it is up to us. *He will never send us away while we are trying to do his will*—even though we may at times do it rather badly— any more than we would disown our own spouses or children for trying to do our will but doing it imperfectly. In other words, the only loophole or uncertainty in the outcome of the gospel contract is on *our* side. It is there to allow *us* a way out of the kingdom if we decide we want out. Those of us who are already in the covenant, but who are still worrying about what *God* is going to do with us in the future, just don't get it. At this point in the relationship it's not up to God anymore—he is *bound* (D&C 82:10). The only uncertainty involved is not what *God* will do (that is certain); rather, it is what *we* will do. We have the option at any time to cancel the contract, to file for divorce by our actions, but God does not—he has committed himself. We can break the agreement, but if we choose not to break it, the outcome is absolutely sure and certain. Thus the ball is in our court, and our destiny is in our own hands.

Our place in the kingdom is ours—ours to keep or ours to lose—but *ours* either way. As Church members, if we want to stay in the kingdom, we can stay. If we want to go, we can go.

It is important to remember that the gate of the kingdom of God is entering the covenant of faith, repentance, baptism, and receiving the gift of the Holy Ghost. If this has already happened to you, then the gates are behind you, and you stand, while faithful, in the kingdom of God. That part of the judgment is already past. Nothing that happens subsequently can be understood as helping you get into the kingdom, or earning your way into the kingdom, or contributing to your getting to the kingdom—because you are already there. It logically follows that for those who have been born again, the critical question is not one of *getting into* the kingdom but of *staying* in the kingdom—of enduring to the end. For we must choose on an ongoing basis to remain, and that choice must be reflected in what we love and in what we seek. That is why enduring to the end is the fifth principle of the gospel. Daily, our question shouldn't be "Have I made it to the kingdom yet?" but rather, "Do I still want to stay?"

I believe that a great key to successfully following

Christ throughout our lives is realizing that we do it as his "born again" sons and daughters (Mosiah 5:7). I personally find great power and comfort in knowing that as I labor for Christ, I labor as a son, encircled in the arms of his love, from a position of safety in his kingdom. I believe that the gratitude and love I feel in response to that knowledge is a stronger motivation for good than fear and anxiety over some future judgment or possible punishment ever could be.

A large part of the good news of the gospel is the promise that the kingdom is ours *now:* "Behold, *the kingdom is yours,* and the enemy shall not overcome" (D&C 38:9, emphasis added; see also D&C 29:5, 35:27, 38:9, 42:69, 45:1, 50:35). Can God lie? Of course not. Then we must accept the fact of our membership in his kingdom *now*—oh, joy and rejoicing!—just as we also accept the duties and chores of sons and daughters in that kingdom. So stop worrying! The hook is set, and if you don't cut the line, there is only *one* possible outcome to your faithful commitment to Christ.

The lifelong choice to stay in the kingdom, to remain in Christ and continue with him in the gospel covenant, is what the scriptures call "enduring faithful to the end." When taken together, *entering* the covenant through faith, repentance, baptism, and receiving the Holy Ghost (believing Christ) and subsequently *staying* in the covenant by enduring faithfully to the end of our lives (following Christ) add up to inheriting celestial glory at the resurrection. Therefore the question is not "Have I made it yet, or not?" The question is "Having been conditionally admitted to the kingdom of God by baptism through the grace of Christ, do I still want to stay? Do I choose to endure?" And as we answer that question honestly, so it shall be.

Chapter Two

ENDURING TO THE END

In the preceding chapter, we saw that whatever "enduring to the end" might be, it's something we are expected to do from a position of strength and safety *within* the kingdom of God, and that we do it to maintain a place there that is already ours by virtue of our covenant in Christ. We are not merely gambling that if we are good enough, we might coax the doors of the kingdom to open for us sometime in the indeterminate future. No, as we endure, we endure as sons and daughters of God who are *already* "encircled in the arms of safety" (Alma 34:16), and knowing that we endure as sons and daughters and as designated heirs ought to make enduring easier. So then, what exactly does it mean to endure to the end? Endure what, and how? And when is the end?

Few promises made in scripture have the credentials and the guarantees of the promise made to those who endure to the end. Take, for example, 3 Nephi 15:9: "Look unto me, and endure to the end, and ye shall live;

for unto him that endureth to the end will I give eternal life." Besides the many prophets who have repeated that promise in the name of God, scripture records both the Father (2 Nephi 31:15, 20) and the Son (3 Nephi 27:16) making the promise directly in the first person. There can simply be no doubt that those who endure to the end will be saved.

For most people, the term *endure* calls up images of tar and feathers or torture on the rack. But few of the Saints are actually faced with such persecutions today. Are we therefore less tested than the Saints of former times? Is it easier for us, with fewer physical trials (collectively speaking), to endure to the end? I think not. In fact, enduring affliction is only the smallest part of what *enduring to the end* really means.

Most frequently the scriptures use the term *endure* to mean "last," "continue," or "remain" rather than "suffer." That is important; it indicates that enduring has more to do with reliability than with stamina. For example, Alma expresses hope that his son Shiblon "will *continue* in keeping [God's] commandments; for blessed is he that *endureth* to the end" (Alma 38:2; emphasis added). Here enduring to the end is explicitly equated with continuing steadfast while in mortality. Nephi had already made that clear in 2 Nephi 33:9: "Be reconciled unto Christ, and enter into the narrow gate, and walk in the strait path which leads to life, and *continue* in the path *until the end* of the day of probation" (emphasis added). Notice that those who have come to Christ have *already* entered into the narrow gate. Now they must continue. Thus to endure means that once we have found the strait and narrow path, we continue in that path (which we adopted at baptism) by keeping our commitments to Christ. First we come to Christ—then we stay put. *Staying put* in the Church and covenant is "enduring." The "end" is the end of our mortal probation (see 2 Nephi 33:9). To endure to the end means we don't let go of Christ; we don't quit the Church and kingdom or lose our testimony because of life's difficulties or temptations—we stay put. Conversely, failing to endure means backing away from what we've started—first promising loyalty to God and his church and then withholding what we've promised, thus proving unreliable and unfaithful. "No man, having put his hand to the plough, *and looking back*, is fit for the kingdom of God" (Luke 9:62; emphasis added). Endurance in the scriptural sense has little to do with physical stamina, for many of the physically most challenged Saints endure like champions as they plow the row God has assigned to them. Rather, endurance is a matter of integrity, of keeping our promises to God once we've been admitted to his covenant and his kingdom.

Just as a spouse who can be trusted to keep the marriage covenant is called faithful, so those who can be trusted to keep their gospel covenants are called faithful. And since the gospel covenant is so often symbolized in scripture as a marriage, it is entirely correct to refer to those who loyally keep that covenant as faithful partners.

In the Old Testament, the words for *faith, faithful,* and *faithfulness* all come from the Hebrew *'aman* (to be firm or reliable) and imply primarily qualities of loyalty and determination rather than qualities of belief. The words for *security, certainty,* and *guarantee* all come from the same Hebrew root. Thus being faithful does not have as much to do with our belief or even our activity in the Church as it does with whether we can be *trusted* to do our duty in the earthly kingdom of God. The covenants of baptism and of the temple are solemn promises we make to God about how we will conduct our lives. Enduring to the end is keeping those promises throughout our lives—no matter what. (However, keeping one's covenants does not mean "never sinning again," since the covenant provides within itself a means of ongoing repentance by partaking of the sacrament.) Unfortunately, due to denominational influence in modern English, the word *faith* has come to be associated primarily with what we believe and largely ignores its original association with *faithfulness.* Thus the modern word *faith* renders only part of the sense of the Hebrew original. If we restore that original nuance (that faith is active commitment to an idea—faithfulness—rather than just passive mental acceptance of it), we largely resolve the false either/or of faith versus works. To have saving faith in Christ is to believe in Christ and to be *faith*ful to Christ. It is to make an investment of ourselves in Christ. It is not enough merely to have a mental conviction that he is the Son of God without letting that conviction have any relevance

to how we live our lives. If we merely believe in his identity without committing our lives to him, then we are no
better than the devils, who also know who he is but are
not benefited by that knowledge (James 2:19).

Usually the scriptures link enduring to the end specifically with remaining faithful to our Christian covenants
and to the covenant community, which is the Church.
For example, D&C 20:29 states: "We know that all men
must repent and believe on the name of Jesus Christ, and
worship the Father in his name, and endure in faith on
his name to the end, or they cannot be saved in the kingdom of God" (see also 2 Nephi 9:24).

The Savior reinforces this covenant dimension of
endurance in his teaching to the Nephites, specifically
emphasizing the covenant obligations of repentance and
baptism: "It shall come to pass, that whoso repenteth and
is baptized in my name shall be filled; and if he endureth
to the end, behold, him will I hold guiltless before my
Father at that day when I shall stand to judge the world"
(3 Nephi 27:16).

So enduring to the end means entering into the gospel
covenant through faith in Christ, repentance, baptism,
and receiving the Holy Ghost and then remaining faithful to that covenant. D&C 20:37 even makes "determination to serve [Christ] to the end" a condition of baptism
into the Church.

Consequently, enduring to the end is more than just
"being active" in the Church. Enduring to the end
requires a personal awareness of covenant obligations and

a personal determination to keep them faithfully. While the term *active* describes visible behavior, *enduring faithful to the end* describes an inner commitment to the gospel and church of Jesus Christ. Of course it's better to be active than inactive, but just being active doesn't guarantee much about our spiritual commitment—even yeast can be "active." We can be active for the wrong reasons, or for trivial reasons. True sons and daughters ought to manage better than yeastcakes. Having a conscious awareness of our covenant obligations and a determination to keep them to the end is being active for the right reasons.

I once knew a man who had to decide whether or not to pay his tithing every time his paycheck came, whether or not to go to his meetings every time they were held, whether or not to take a drink every time he was offered one. Finally I asked him, "Why can't you just decide once and for all which side you're on? Why do you have to double-check your loyalty every time a decision is called for? You are spiritually reinventing the wheel over and over again, and you will never make any progress until you can build on what you already know." A few weeks later he called and asked for a ride to our stake meetings. I was pleased he was going, and when I told him so, he responded, "You know, I wouldn't like it if my wife told me she had to decide every morning whether she still loved me or not, or if she told me she only stayed with me because she hadn't found a good enough reason to leave—yet. I guess the Lord is entitled to more of a commitment than that from me. I'm ready to stop reinventing the wheel and move on with my life. I've decided that I'm ready once and for all to *be* a Latter-day Saint."

Some people are basically saying "Well, *today* I think the Church is true, but ask me again tomorrow." But there must come some point at which our commitment to the gospel and our conviction of its truth settles such questions in advance and predetermines our response *to whatever challenge we may encounter to our faith, to whatever commandments we may receive, or to whatever sacrifice we are called upon to make.*[1] That isn't blind faith; rather, it's a vague suspicion that has finally managed to *become* true faith! Faith, after all, is spiritual knowledge—not a guess, not a hunch, not a hope, but knowledge. Most often it is knowledge unsupported by physical evidence or even challenged by the available evidence. Until our faith has a life and a strength of its own apart from intellectual argument or even physical evidence, it is not yet faith. In such cases what we thought was faith was merely the strongest human argument we had considered at the time. A testimony isn't like a hypothesis in science, which may be supported by the evidence one day and destroyed by it the next. It is a conviction *beyond* the available intellectual proof that some things are eternally true. The "provisionally converted"

---

[1] See JST Luke 14:38, where the Savior counsels the disciples, "*Settle* this in your hearts, that ye will do the things which I shall teach and command you" (emphasis added).

are those who have not received such a conviction (or who will not accept it) but who haven't found a good enough reason to leave—yet. Just as such a low level of commitment is unsatisfactory in a marriage, so in the long run it is unsatisfactory in the spiritual marriage of the gospel. Such people need to become converted and let the question of the truth of the gospel be *decided*, once and for all, by the witness of the Spirit. Just as a celestial marriage says, "We are sealed, no matter what," so a truly converted member says, "I am a member of this church, and my lot is cast with the apostles and prophets—no matter what. Above all other issues, loyalties, agendas, and commitments, *this* is where I stand; *this* is what I believe; *this* is whom I serve." Then and only then can we experience the power and the blessings promised to the faithful.

Without such a prior commitment, some new commandment or sacrifice or some imagined (or real) offense on the part of Church leaders might challenge our endurance. It is possible to be an "active" member of the Church without such a conviction, but it may not be possible to endure to the end. The Lord spoke of those who could not make such a commitment in the Parable of the Sower—they have no root in themselves but endure only for a while; then, when difficulties arise because of the word, eventually they are offended (Matthew 13:21). We must not fear to send our roots deep—deep into the gospel and deep into the Church, for it is just as self-destructive spiritually for us to hold back part of our promised loyalty as it was for Ananias and Sapphira to hold back part of their promised offerings (Acts 5:1–11).[2]

According to the scriptures, besides remaining faithful to our baptismal covenants, other component parts of enduring faithful to the end include:

1. Looking unto Christ (3 Nephi 15:9).

2. Continuing to take upon us the name of Christ (3 Nephi 27:6).

3. Feasting upon the words of Christ in steadfastness, hope, and love (2 Nephi 31:20; Moroni 8:26).

4. Offering our whole souls to Christ in fasting and prayer (Omni 1:26).

5. Following the example of Christ (2 Nephi 31:16).

6. Worshipping the Father in the name of Christ (D&C 20:29).

7. Keeping the commandments (1 Nephi 22:31; Alma 38:2; D&C 14:7).

8. Seeking to bring forth Zion with patience and humility (1 Nephi 13:37; Alma 32:15; D&C 24:8).

Notice that the common focus of all of these scriptural exhortations to endurance is not primarily *suffering* but *loyalty* to Christ.

Often those who cannot keep their commitments seek to justify themselves by separating loyalty to Christ from loyalty to his church, but that is impossible. Our

---

[2]See also the examples of those who heard Jesus' "Bread of Life" sermon and were content to believe in him when he fed them but who were offended and "walked no more with him" when he taught them hard doctrines (John 6).

covenants in the restored gospel of Christ are covenants that specifically include our relationship with his church and that are administered through his church—The Church of Jesus Christ of Latter-day Saints. *We cannot endure to the end in those covenants without enduring to the end in that church.* That is made clear by the Savior himself: "Whosoever is *of my church*, and endureth *of my church* to the end, him will I establish upon my rock, and the gates of hell shall not prevail against them" (D&C 10:69; emphasis added).[3]

There are no side bets or private arrangements. Enduring in our covenants means enduring *in the Church*. God will not excuse those who leave the Church thinking that they have good reasons or that they can keep covenants made in and through the Church while rejecting the Church or fighting with the Church. No matter what their intentions, they are deceived. By definition, if they have not lasted, they have failed to endure to the end. And there is no acceptable substitute for the covenant relationship outside the church and kingdom of God upon the earth.

WHAT DOES IT MEAN TO BE "FAITHFUL"?

A common error made by some members of the Church is to equate the faithfulness that is part of enduring to the end with being sinless. Every time we commit a sin, they would argue, we are unfaithful to Christ and

---

[3]See also D&C 50:8 and 85:11.

violate our covenants. But that will not wash at all, for *all* the faithful Saints continue to commit sins from time to time. That is why the repentance and renewal associated with the ordinance of the sacrament is *part* of the gospel covenant. God has *anticipated* that his sons and daughters within the Church and within the covenant will mess up more or less regularly, and he has provided us with a remedy when we do.

Just as faithful spouses may not be perfect and may do things that injure their partners and wound the relationship without necessarily ending the marriage, so faithful Church members are also imperfect and may do things that stress their covenant relationship with God—without necessarily ending that relationship. I'm not arguing here that such mistakes are trivial or that they don't matter. I'm only arguing that they don't necessarily terminate the covenant. What does it mean when my wife, Janet, rolls her eyes and says, "Oh well, at least he's faithful"? She certainly *doesn't* mean that I'm perfect! Rather she means that despite my many flaws, I am loyal to her— there is no one else. Similarly, in the gospel covenant, being faithful doesn't mean being perfect. It just means we're loyal to Christ, and there is nobody else (no interest, cause, or loyalty ahead of him). In our own covenants with each other, we can distinguish between being perfect on the one hand and being faithful on the other. True, some evil acts violate the marriage covenant and leave it in ruins, but forgetting a wedding anniversary isn't one of them. Similarly, some evil acts violate the gospel covenant and put us outside the kingdom, but swearing in traffic isn't one of them. That is why the Lord has instructed us to meet often to partake of the sacrament— to repent of the sins he knows we commit and thus to renew our covenants. We "renew" them because they get soiled and tattered in our day-to-day lives—because we make mistakes and need to get back to base. Still, as long as Christ comes first in our lives, as long as we haven't made him second to some other "love," then we are still faithful partners, though we may need to apologize to him from time to time and start over in some areas of our relationship. As long as we are in mortality, we will have the need to repent and renew our covenants regularly. But that does not mean we are unfaithful—not unless some other loyalty, some other love, has taken Christ's place as our highest concern.

By way of illustration, perhaps you can imagine a second-string soccer goalie who has average ability but who isn't as good as the fellow who plays in front of him. So most of the time he just sits on the bench. Is he off the team because he doesn't start? No, he's on the team; he just isn't the most talented member at that position right now. Now suppose that because of injuries to the one who plays in front of him, this second-string goalie gets into the big game, where he does an okay job, and his team wins—even though he allowed three goals. Is he on the *other* team now because he allowed the opposition to score three times and a better goalie wouldn't have? When the game is over, should his teammates treat him as a traitor for his errors? Because his limited talent worked in their favor, does the other team owe him something? Of course not. Our second-string goalie may lack talent, but there is no question about his loyalty or about which team he's on. Playing our best game and making mistakes does not put us off the team. We may sit on the bench for our mistakes—but we aren't the enemy.

Similarly, in the church and kingdom of God some players have more talent at some positions than others; some have more strength or experience than others. Not everyone can be relied upon to perform well at every position or in every circumstance. That does not make them unfaithful, and it doesn't mean they are off the team. They are merely the second string right now. Their desire to serve Christ, to repent regularly and improve steadily, guarantees they are still in the kingdom. They are on the right side—even if they're not the most talented players at their position right now. And we in the Church must learn to separate the issue of strength and talent from the issue of loyalty and faithfulness, both in our own self-evaluations and in the way we judge others.[4]

On the other hand, suppose that before the game the *first* team goalie had met with the opposing team and been paid to let them score. Whom does he serve? To

---

[4]We also need to learn the difference, as Elder Dallin Oaks has pointed out, between "mistakes" and "sins" (see Dallin Oaks, "Sins and Mistakes," BYU Campus Education Week, August 1994).

whom does he belong? Even though his skills may be superior, he serves a different master than his teammates serve, and his disloyalty does make him the enemy. But just being a klutz won't do it.

Some of us are too quick to assume that we are the second- and third-string players or that we are spiritual klutzes. We forget that God, in his perfect judgment, adjusts credit and blame to allow for the circumstances of the individual in question. The gospel is not a "one-size-fits-all" arrangement in that regard. God puts us all in different circumstances in this life and judges us accordingly. In the Parable of the Talents, it didn't matter that one servant had been given five talents and the other only two. What mattered most was what both servants did with what God gave them. The Master said to *each* of them, "Well done, thou good and faithful servant" (Matthew 25:21). It is better to be a faithful second-string player with limited talents (pun intended) than to be an unfaithful superstar.

THE PARABLE OF THE DIVERS

Many years ago, when I was somewhere between nine and eleven, I participated in a community summer recreation program in the town where I grew up. I remember in particular a diving competition for the different age groups held at the community swimming pool. Some of the wealthier kids in our area had their own pools with diving boards, and they were pretty good amateur divers. But there was one kid my age from the less affluent part of town who didn't have his own pool. What he had was raw courage. While the rest of us did our crisp little swan dives, back dives, and jackknives, being ever so careful to arch our backs and point our toes, this young man attempted back flips, one-and-a-halfs, doubles, and so on. But, oh, he was sloppy. He seldom kept his feet together, he never pointed his toes, and he usually missed his vertical entry. The rest of us observed with smug satisfaction as the judges held up their scorecards that he consistently got lower marks than we did with our safe and simple dives, and we congratulated ourselves that we were actually the better divers. "He is all heart and no finesse," we told ourselves. "After all, *we* keep *our* feet together and point *our* toes."

The announcement of the winners was a great shock to us, for the brave young lad with the flips had apparently beaten us all. However, I had kept rough track of the scores in my head, and I knew with the arrogance of limited information that the math didn't add up. I had consistently outscored the boy with the flips. And so, certain that an injustice was being perpetrated, I stormed the scorer's table and demanded an explanation. "Degree of difficulty," the scorer replied matter-of-factly as he looked me in the eye. "Sure, you had better form, but he did harder dives. When you factor in the degree of difficulty, he beat you hands down, kid." Until that moment I hadn't known that some dives were awarded "extra credit" because of their greater difficulty.

I have a friend to whom life has been unkind. Though

she married in the temple, her husband proved unfaithful and eventually abandoned her and their small children. Since he has never paid a penny in child support, my friend works full time to support herself and her kids. For several years she also went to school at night to improve her financial situation. Therefore, of necessity, she could not be with her children as much as she would have liked and could not always give them the guidance and discipline they needed. It just wasn't possible in her difficult circumstances. One result of her less-than-perfect family situation was troubled teenagers. Now in middle age she is faced with raising some of her grandchildren—again, all alone. Without a faithful companion, without the priesthood in her home, without the blessings that are realized where the ideal family setting is possible, it is almost inevitable that my friend should feel that her "scores" as a wife and mother, and perhaps even as a person, aren't very high. When she goes to church and sees other "ideal" LDS families, when she hears them bear their testimonies and give thanks for all their spiritual and temporal blessings, she sees in her mind the judges holding up scorecards that say 9.9 or 10.0. When she looks at her own life, her own failed marriage, her own troubled children, she knows that the scores are much lower, and she worries about her place in the kingdom.

Well, she needn't worry, for she is as faithful to her covenants in her troubles as the rest of us are in our blessings. True, there are some things she *cannot* do, but these are the result of her circumstances, not choices pursued by her own free will, and where there is no choice, there can be no condemnation. I have no doubt that when the "degree of difficulty" is factored in for the life she leads, her crown will shine brighter than many others, for God always factors into his judgments the "degree of difficulty."[5]

Whenever I am tempted to feel superior to other Saints, the parable of the divers comes to my mind, and I repent. At least at a swim meet, we can usually tell which dives are the most difficult. But here in mortality, we cannot always tell who is carrying what burdens: limited intelligence, chemical depression, compulsive behaviors, learning disabilities, dysfunctional or abusive family background, poor health, physical or psychological handicaps—no one chooses these things. So I must not judge my brothers and sisters. I am thankful for my blessings but not smug about them, for I *never* want to hear the Scorer say to me, "Sure, you had better form, but she had a harder life. When you factor in degree of difficulty, she beat you hands down."

So, enduring to the end doesn't have much to do with suffering in silence, overcoming all life's obstacles, or even achieving the LDS ideal ("pointing our toes" and "keeping our feet together"). It just means not giving up. It means keeping—to the best of our abilities—the

---

[5]See D&C 82:3. If much is required where much is given, then where less is given (two talents rather than five), less must be required. Also, see Luke 21:1–4 where the widow's mite was judged to be more in God's eyes than the rich endowments of the wealthy.

commitments we made to Christ when we entered into the marriage of the gospel. It means not divorcing the Savior or cheating on him by letting some other love become more important in our lives. It means not rejecting the blessings of the atonement that he showered upon us when we entered his church and kingdom.

FAITHFULNESS AND REPENTANCE

The process of recognizing the carnal self as carnal and its desires as often contrary to God's will, then denying the carnal self and complying with God's will, is called repentance. The Hebrew word for *repent* is *shuv*, and it means literally "to turn," that is, to turn from following the carnal self and begin following Christ instead.

One problem some Saints seem prone to in their understanding of repentance is that they want to see repentance as an event rather than a lifestyle. Though repentance is required before baptism can take place, it is not once-and-for-all repentance that must take place at that time. That would be impossible, for repentance is intended to be a continuing lifestyle, a way of conducting ourselves as we follow Christ. Just as we do not have faith and then stop having it once we are baptized, so we do not repent just once and then stop repenting after we are baptized—faith and repentance must *both* continue even after baptism. Ongoing repentance is a necessary part of following Christ and being faithful to our covenants.

First, the Lord has directed that we partake of the

sacrament regularly to renew our covenants. The steps of faith and repentance that precede baptism also precede this ordinance, and partaking of the sacrament in this manner can have the same spiritual effect as being baptized again. If we could repent once and for all before baptism and put all sin behind us forever, there would be no need for the frequent renewal of our covenants and commitment by partaking of the sacrament.

Second, since our goal is the perfect righteousness of the Father and the Son, and since we cannot achieve this entirely in mortality, *as long as we live* we're going to have something to repent of, some error to correct, something to work on or eliminate from our lives in order to be more like God. Those who say they do not need continuing repentance are either unaware of their sins or covering for them. Since individual perfection (unlike perfection in Christ) is impossible in mortality (Romans 3:23), there will always be something to repent of. Thus repentance is a process that must begin in earnest at conversion but continue to improve us and bring us closer to God all our lives. We can never be *done* repenting until we have become what he is. In that sense, repentance is an attitude, an attitude of recognizing our sins, then rejecting them in principle, then working to get rid of them in fact. As we succeed in recognizing and removing big sins like violence, immorality, or a bad temper, we can progress to medium sins like selfishness, ingratitude, and laziness. Hopefully, we can eventually get to the smaller sins like being late to church or not singing when we get there.

Since repenting is "turning" ourselves around, I think a useful analogy can be drawn from the navy. When a captain decides to turn a battleship or an aircraft carrier, it takes some time for the ship to come around. Though the decision has been made, the order has been given, and the change is being carried out, it still takes some *time* to bring a ship about. So in our lives the decisions for Christ can be truly and genuinely made, the order truly given and carried out, yet it can still take some time and space to overcome the natural resistance of the carnal self and make the complete turn. There will be rejoicing when the turn is completed and we have perfected part or all of our lives, but should we die before it's done, the Lord will still credit us for making the right decision, for issuing the appropriate orders and attempting to carry them out in our lives—the rest would have been just a matter of time. If we should die, as all of us do, with some sins not completely eliminated, it will not harm us. God will give us credit for what we would have accomplished given more time (D&C 137:7–8). Were we truly repentant? Did we truly desire to root sin out of our lives? Then we are justified through the atonement of Christ and will eventually achieve what we sought in life.

THE "MIGHTY CHANGE"

Surely someone, perhaps one of the spiritual masochists among us (or spiritual sadists—we have both in the

Church), is going to object, "But what about 'the mighty change?' Did not the Spirit work a mighty change within the people of Benjamin so that they had *'no more disposition to do evil, but to do good continually'?"* (Mosiah 5:2). That is true, but what is being described there is a change in disposition, a change of desire, a change in our compass headings. From the moment of their conversion (or reconversion), the people of Benjamin changed their orientation and wanted righteousness rather than wickedness. It became their one goal. But that does *not* mean they achieved their goal instantaneously! It does *not* mean they never had another carnal thought or that they never subsequently lost any struggle against their carnal natures. At that moment, filled with the Spirit and clearly seeing the two paths before them, the people of Benjamin lost all desire to follow the path of evil. I feel the same way when I feel the Spirit, but I do not always feel the Spirit. And as with Moses, when the epiphany (divine appearance) is over, Satan sometimes takes his best shot (Moses 1:9–12). Therefore we must recharge our spiritual batteries regularly.

Great spiritual damage can be done by teaching the Saints that "the mighty change" means once truly converted we are never again tempted to sin. For if the Saints believe that the *truly* converted are never subsequently tempted, then when they are tempted—and they will be—they will conclude they are not really converted. However, being truly converted does not end the tests of mortality, for we will continue to be tested and tempted as long as we are in the flesh. Even as covenant members of the church of Jesus Christ, we will continue to be subject to the carnal impulses and other weaknesses that are a consequence of the Fall.

Since my own conversion, if at any time an angel had somehow presented me with two options and said, "Push button A and you will never sin again; push button B and you will," I'd have pushed button A—without hesitation and hard enough to break my thumb! Imperfect as I am, since my conversion I in fact "have no more disposition to do evil but to do good continually," and neither do most of us. It's just that we have difficulty overcoming our carnal natures and the effects of the Fall at all times in order to act according to our predisposition. That our disposition is *good* is proven by the fact that when we occasionally act otherwise, we feel bad about it, repent, and return to our previous heading toward righteousness. Like a compass needle that may swing this way or that but always comes again to point north, so are the believers who may make this or that temporary misstep but always correct their course and return to their original heading. That is a clear disposition to do good. "The mighty change" is a change of heart, a change of desires, and a change of disposition concerning our goals. It is not a complete victory over the Fall or over our carnal natures all at once.

Chapter Three

THE FALL OF ADAM AND EVE

It would be difficult to understand the good news of the gospel and particularly of the atonement of Christ without first understanding the *bad* news about the fall of Adam and Eve, for it is the Fall and its consequences that make the Atonement necessary.[1] As the Fall separates us from God, so the Atonement reunites us with God. Therefore, without the Fall, the gospel would be unnecessary—like a hospital in a world where no one got sick or injured. The Fall is the problem to which the Atonement is the solution.

Indeed, those occasions when we most eagerly turn to God are often the times when we are confronted most directly by the effects of the Fall. For example, when we or our loved ones are sick or dying, we turn to God to

---

[1]As President Ezra Taft Benson said, "No one adequately and properly knows why he needs Christ until he understands and accepts the doctrine of the Fall and its effect upon all mankind" (*A Witness and A Warning* [Deseret Book: Salt Lake City, 1988], p. 33).

plead for help. We may not realize that we are asking him to remove certain effects of the Fall in our behalf, but that is what we are doing. Similarly, when we pray for forgiveness of sins, or for help when we can't overcome life's obstacles, or for guidance when we don't know the right thing to do—we are praying for deliverance from specific aspects of the Fall or from its natural consequences. Too many of us think of our problems as individual symptoms without understanding the underlying cause of our condition. We talk about "health problems," "I.Q. problems," "lack of willpower," or "trouble controlling my thoughts" without realizing that these are just isolated symptoms of a bigger problem—the fall of the human race.

We must also understand the Fall in order to know our limitations here in mortality. Without fully appreciating the limitations placed upon us by the Fall, many of the Saints have despaired because they can't overcome all things on their own or all at once. But given our true circumstances here in mortality, such expectations are wildly unrealistic. As we strive to endure to the end, we will do better if we know what our handicaps are. We need to know what we can reasonably expect to accomplish on our own and what we must rely on the Savior to overcome for us through his love and mercy. For example, it would be silly of me to expect that if I am righteous enough I can overcome old age or death, for victory over these enemies (though guaranteed) comes only later on and through Christ. And there are other enemies we similarly cannot hope to overcome right now or on our own. These impediments are all associated with the fall of Adam and Eve.

While the great victory of Jesus Christ over all our enemies has already been won, the natural effects of the Fall are nevertheless allowed to continue with us, and will continue until the Savior comes again to assert his ultimate lordship. Thus, while ultimate victory over our enemies is certain through Jesus Christ and in fact has already been won, we still have to wrestle with those enemies during our mortal lives. God intends that we struggle under these handicaps and limitations, for that is part of the test of mortality.

The truth is that we humans in our natural state are *all* in trouble—deep, deep trouble. Because of the Fall, we are caught in the "no-win" situation called mortality.[2] In this condition we are vulnerable to many enemies (Satan, sin, death, hell, disease, error, and so on) and require the help of God to get out of their power and ultimately out of the trap altogether. The foolish among us make the connection between God's redeeming power and our individual mortal problems only when some aspect of the Fall actually has us in its teeth, like sickness or death. But that is what the gospel is all about—becoming aware of our true situation and our truly desperate

---

[2]That is, "no-win" without the atonement of Christ. As I discuss the bad news here, I am excluding that obvious solution because we need to know the problem in order to appreciate the answer.

circumstances (the results of the Fall) and then learning how this situation and these circumstances can be overcome forever (through the atonement of Christ).

MORTALITY IS NOT OUR PROPER ELEMENT

It stands to reason that if we are fallen, then we must be fallen *from* someplace. We did not begin in a world like the one we now live in, nor is this natural world our proper setting. As spirit children of God, we first lived with heavenly parents in a glory to which we now hope to return. In a sense, we are fallen from those celestial courts on high and are now looking for the ladder back up. Also, when our first parents were created physically on this earth, they were created in a more glorified state than that we now experience, a condition roughly equivalent to a terrestrial glory, in which no one suffered or died. God created Adam and Eve nonmortal and immune to suffering, but these pleasant physical conditions changed for the worse with the Fall.[3] Thus humanity has digressed by degrees from the celestial, premortal world of our heavenly parents to the terrestrial Eden, and from thence has fallen hard to this telestial condition. In his redemptive work, Christ will reverse the process, first restoring the earth to its terrestrial or paradisiacal glory (the glory associated with Eden) and then after the

---

[3]Technically, Adam and Eve were *a*mortal rather than *im*mortal. Amortal means one is not presently subject to death, although under certain circumstances one could be. Immortal means one is immune to death under any circumstances.

Millennium raising earth to its ultimate celestial glory (Article of Faith 10; Revelation 21:1–2; D&C 77:1–2).

Nevertheless, the Fall was neither a tragedy nor a mistake but a necessary step in the eternal progress of God's spirit children, for we had reached the point in our premortal growth where it was time to meet the opposition in a mortal setting, to encounter the evil and negative elements of existence, and to be sorted out according to our response to that opposition. Mortality is the sorting shed. Here some of us will pursue light most of the time no matter what the cost; some will pursue light some of the time if it doesn't cost too much; and others will prefer darkness. Unfortunately, our *real* preferences can be fairly tested only on a level playing floor, that is, in a place where light and darkness, good and evil, are both readily available to us equally, "for it must needs be, that there is an opposition in all things" (2 Nephi 2:11). Mortality is designed to offer those conditions. Mortal life is like an all-you-can-eat buffet dinner with all the moral options spread out before us, from the pure, the virtuous, the righteous, and the holy at one end of the table to the abominable, the wicked, the corrupt, and the vile at the other end. Pick what you like; eat all you want; but your choices will unmistakably reveal what you prefer and therefore what you are. When we can have all we want of whatever we want, our choices unerringly reveal our true character. In this analogy, you are what you eat. In real life, you are what you *choose*.

However, the environment necessary for this test,

this buffet dinner with good and evil presented on the same table, with the opposition present in all things, could not be created in the presence of God, for "no unclean thing can . . . dwell in his presence" (Moses 6:57). (Mom can't know I'm trustworthy until I've been left *alone* with the cookie jar. As long as she's watching, it's not a fair test.) Therefore, in order to be enticed equally by the evil as well as by the good, it was necessary for us to leave home, to descend from that exalted place of our spirit birth and come into a world like this one—neutral ground for a fair test. Here we can't even tell we *have* parents, let alone whether they're watching us or not.[4]

Since the Fall (the separation from God that allows us to be enticed equally by both good and evil) was necessary to human progress rather than being a tragic misstep, in fact since God fully *intended* that the Fall take place, it would be grossly unfair for God to punish Adam and Eve for it. After all, the Garden of Eden was pretty much a setup for the Fall to occur. For that reason, after Adam and Eve were cast out, God forgave them their transgression in the Garden of Eden and absolved them of any blame for it (Moses 6:53). They were assured they would not be blamed for what occurred before the Fall nor for the Fall itself. Rather, since the Fall was part of God's plan, all its negative aspects would unconditionally and unilaterally be canceled out for them and their posterity through the grace of God and the atonement of Jesus

---

[4]Except, of course, by faith.

Christ, who alone would bear the burden of the Fall. I hope the reader perceives the wonderful fairness here: since the Fall was part of God's plan, God and God alone will assume all its permanent costs and burdens.

For that reason several Church leaders have insisted on a difference in kind between the "transgression" of Adam and Eve in the Garden of Eden and sins committed after the Fall.[5] After all, the "transgression" was committed under duress in the "setup" in the Garden with its extremely limited options, was committed without Adam and Eve having full moral understanding or accountability,[6] was necessary for the further progress of God's plan, and was fully intended by God to be the outcome of the Eden experience. It was therefore forgiven them unilaterally through the atonement of Christ. That is only fair.

However, those sins committed by Adam and Eve and their posterity *after* the Fall, by their own free choice and with full knowledge and accountability, can be forgiven only through the atonement of Christ by entering into the gospel covenant—also by our own free choice. Please note the parallel: The negative effects of the Fall that came about *without* our participation (sickness, death, and so on) are also canceled *without* our participation.

---

[5]See Joseph Fielding Smith, *Doctrines of Salvation* 1:112–15 or Bruce R. McConkie, *Mormon Doctrine* (Bookcraft: Salt Lake City, 1966), p. 804.

[6]They had not yet partaken of the fruit of knowledge of good and evil.

The negative effects brought about *with* our participation (our own sins) are canceled only *with* our participation in the gospel covenant.

FAMILIAR ASPECTS OF THE FALL

So how does the fall of Adam and Eve still affect us? As their physical offspring, we inherit the physical consequences of their actions just as we inherit their changed physical condition. The offspring of Adam and Eve are fallen physically. That may not be apparent to people in their twenties who are enjoying good health, but when we are sick or injured and as we age, the evidence becomes more clear—to be born is also to suffer and die. There is no more inexorable connection, no more firmly established scientific certainty in the natural world than that. The bad news here is particularly bad: at some point in your life, whatever is wrong with you will get worse, and then you'll die.

However, that particular aspect of the Fall doesn't usually take us all at once. First, the teeth get cavities, the waistline thickens, the knees go bad, the hair falls out. First we need glasses, then stronger prescriptions, then bifocals, then trifocals. We don't often think of the dentist, the optometrist, or the toupé-maker as helping us cope with the effects of the Fall, but that is what they do. Moreover, physicians, nurses, pharmacists, psychiatrists, psychologists, physical therapists, lab technicians, dietitians, and manufacturers of vitamins, health foods, exercise bikes, and stair-steppers—all these and many more occupations exist only to help us briefly hold at bay the effects of the Fall. But no one can stop the process, for funeral directors, morticians, and gravediggers are also in the "Fall" business and are its ultimate and inevitable conclusion in this world. While death is the most dramatic evidence of our physically fallen state, we should not forget that injury, sickness, pain—all the physical problems with which humans suffer—are also results of our being fallen. In Eden it was not so, nor will it be when Christ restores again to this earth its paradisiacal glory.

Besides being physically fallen, we are also spiritually fallen. That can be correctly described as geographical separation from God, being physically excluded from his presence because of our fallen and sinful condition (Moses 5:4). But the spiritual aspects of the Fall are more directly experienced as feelings of loneliness, inadequacy, alienation, anxiety, depression, and guilt. Where once we lived and talked with heavenly parents for thousands, perhaps millions, of years, suddenly we have been separated from that divine influence. What comfort, what security must our parents have given us as we grew up under their loving care. How much a part of our lives they must have become in those premortal aeons. Now, like homesick freshmen, we suffer from a tremendous separation anxiety, a sense of loss brought about by the Fall, but because the veil has been drawn over our minds, we cannot remember what it is that we so desperately miss. The resulting condition might be called severe spiritual trauma, like being hit on the head, kidnapped, and waking up as a slave with amnesia in Timbuktu. In our spiritually more sensitive moments, we may feel that something isn't quite right about all this, but until we find and accept the gospel of Jesus Christ we can't really know what is wrong with this life or how to fix it. Somewhere deep within us, we grieve for the loss of a home and a life we cannot remember. We only feel the loss in our bones.

OTHER ASPECTS OF THE FALL

While the physical and spiritual aspects of the Fall, death, and separation from God get a lot of attention, I would like to point out some other aspects that are often overlooked but that also have a profound impact on us here in mortality. For example, we often forget that as fallen beings we are *mentally* fallen.

We humans trust reason and logic; some of us trust reason more than we trust God. We have a tendency to think that if we start with what we know to be true and proceed with correct logic, we will always arrive at correct conclusions, but that is wrong, for human reason is flawed—it is fallen. First of all, we can't ever start from what we already know, because we start here on earth knowing nothing. We bring no data with us from behind the veil. We may have intuitive flashes, and some things we encounter may have a familiar feel, but we have no empirical data, no rational memories from our pre-earth life. We start out with a blank tape. Only the gospel gives us guaranteed data to start from and a guaranteed perspective from which to interpret it.

Second, even if fallen reason did have reliable data to start with, we couldn't follow it through to correct conclusions, for intellect itself is a defective instrument. If a yardstick that is too long or too short is always used to measure *itself* when it is checked, the error will never be detected. Since intellect is our fallen yardstick, intellect can never detect its own distortions. Most of us are aware that our universe keeps surprising us, that it resists our attempts to impose our understanding upon it. We live daily with the bloody noses that result from the way things *really* are being different from the way we *suppose* them to be. These are practical lessons in the inability of human intellect to deal infallibly with mortal reality. If we don't maintain a certain humility, and therefore a certain caution, about our ability to reason correctly and thereby to control our own fate, life will wound us dearly. And we are most at risk when we are most sure of ourselves.

Experience and common sense perceive the effects of the Fall all around us, even though that perception may not always be connected with religious thinking. For example, one popular recognition of our fallen situation is voiced in Murphy's Law: "If things can go wrong they will, and probably already have." That bit of folk wisdom correctly recognizes the "friction" or opposition that the Fall adds to our existence. The same idea is contained in the popular maxim "Stuff happens." Though not overtly religious, both of these popular formulas describe the actual, perceptible effects of the Fall in human affairs.

The Scottish poet Robert Burns similarly noted these limitations of mortality when he wrote, "The best-laid schemes o' mice an' men gang aft agley."[7] Though staunch humanists—even in the Church—will naively argue to the contrary, we humans are not able to control our destinies by our reason alone, for our reason is fallen and defective and will lead us into errors: "The natural man receiveth not the things of the Spirit of God: for they are foolishness unto him: neither can he know them, because they are spiritually discerned. . . . For the wisdom of this world is foolishness with God" (1 Corinthians 2:14; 3:19). If we are ever to detect and rise above the distortions of our fallen intellect, we need another yardstick—a correct one—to measure our reason by, and that yardstick is the revealed gospel of Jesus Christ.

Much of the time, even most of the time, relying on our best reasoning is a sound operating procedure—most of the time it's the best we've got—but it must always be tempered with the humility that comes from understanding the effects of the Fall on our reason. Fallen intellect can't get things right, not completely. *Fallen intellect can never arrive at the whole truth on its own.* Thus those who rely on intellect and human reasoning alone as their surest guides in this life are doomed to be "ever learning but never able to come to a knowledge of the truth." They have a self-verifying—but nevertheless

---

[7]That is, "go oft awry." From Burns's poem "To a Mouse on Turning Her Up in Her Nest with the Plough."

54

defective—yardstick. Only the gospel gives us a reliable indication of when we are working beyond our rational limitations. Only a *revealed* yardstick can be used to check the calibrations of human wisdom, for the false yardstick of human wisdom will always validate itself when used to measure itself. Absent the influence of the Holy Ghost on some level (whether as revelation, inspiration, intuition, or whatever), our reason will eventually lead us into error.

Another way in which we are fallen is emotionally. Our emotions, like our flesh, are part of our carnal natures. They are flawed and often out of control. We cannot choose our temperament. We don't usually choose what will "bug" us. Sometimes our emotional state can be influenced by physical or chemical factors in the brain, and in these cases may not be governed by agency or subject to accountability. However, in most cases our fallen emotions, like our fallen bodies, can and must be subjected to the rule of our spirits. Moreover, we can't very well choose whom or what to love or determine how intensely we will love them. If we have too much of the wrong kind of contact, our emotions can create new attachments or dissolve old ones when we didn't intend for that to happen. Our emotions are a poor substitute for the Spirit as a guide in our lives, and to follow our unbridled emotions is as foolish as to follow our unbridled flesh. I express it as my opinion that in the resurrection, our emotions, if we have subjected them to our spirits, will no longer be out of control, will no longer be fallen, but will be subject to our will. They will then be as God's emotions are—always under control and always redemptive in their expression.

Also we are fallen morally. That means our sense of right and wrong is defective. While it may be true that we can usually let our conscience be our guide, many times different individuals get contradictory indications from their consciences, and often conscience does not state any opinion whatsoever. The desire to do the right thing doesn't help much if we don't know what the right thing is. The light of Christ gives all people enough information to be held accountable for some sins, and perhaps to avoid certain sins, but it cannot be a substitute for the Holy Ghost. The light of Christ does not have sufficient intensity to serve as a guide for all people in all circumstances—especially if a fallen reason and a carnal nature are urging us in a different direction. Yet mortality requires us to make complex moral judgments about what is right and wrong. In the absence of the gift of the Holy Spirit, we will simply come to the wrong conclusions, and we may even do it while thinking we are right.

The total effect of being fallen in all these ways (physically, spiritually, mentally, emotionally, and morally) is to make the test of mortality much more difficult. At the same time, we receive a physical body, which *naturally* seeks pleasure rather than righteousness because it has no ability to distinguish between right and wrong—flesh has no conscience. I mean that literally. Just as a thermometer cannot detect radiation and a Geiger counter cannot detect heat, so our flesh cannot detect light and truth—it wasn't designed to do it. Flesh can distinguish only between pleasure and pain, between "feels good" and "doesn't feel good," and therefore it urges us to act upon that distinction alone. The unredeemed carnal self, our flesh and its desires, readily serves the devil because it has no moral sense, no spiritual discernment, and no conscience. It was not designed that way—the ability to make those distinctions was given to our spirit. Unredeemed and without the guidance of spirit, our flesh is morally blind and is therefore an enemy to God, for Satan can successfully argue to the flesh that sin is *pleasurable* even when he can't successfully argue to the spirit that sin is *right*. Consequently, being both incredibly powerful and morally blind, until and unless the carnal self yields to the enticing of the Holy Spirit and accepts the leadership of our own spirit with its moral vision, it remains a loose cannon and an enemy to God (Mosiah 3:19).

But please note that we do not seek to destroy or escape the flesh or the carnal self but rather to subject it to the Spirit and to sanctify it. The capacity for pleasure is not, after all, evil. It is necessary and desirable—not when it is our highest priority but rather when it accepts the leadership of the Spirit and serves the interests of the Spirit.

Since we are not perfected all at once when we are converted, we ought not to expect that the carnal self will be subjected to the spirit all at once either. Just as those who have been redeemed from death through the

Atonement and Resurrection still have to die anyway, so those who have overcome the carnal self through the Atonement still have to wrestle with it anyway.

In the worst cases, the carnal self can be horribly, leeringly wicked. In the best cases, the carnal self can also be human beings just doing the best they know how—without God—and getting it all wrong as a result. As even the truly converted attempt to follow Christ, they should not suppose they will be freed immediately from every influence of the carnal self. Struggling with that self is part of the test, and our test is not yet over. Indeed, the process of refinement will last more than our lifetime. Victory is assured to the faithful through the atonement of Christ (1 John 5:4–5; D&C 38:7–9), but our individual struggle continues as long as we are in the flesh.

The final bit of bad news is that since the Fall subjects us to a carnal nature, it also puts us at increased risk of personal sin. The Fall is not in itself the immediate *cause* of our personal sins, but it does put us in a bad neighborhood where we may encounter and be enticed by sin. That enticement, combined with the enthusiastic urging of our carnal self, often overcomes the righteous desires of our spirit, and we pollute ourselves.[8]

---

[8]This is the meaning of Moses 6:55: "Inasmuch as thy children are conceived in sin, even so when they begin to grow up, sin conceiveth in their hearts, and they taste the bitter, that they may know to prize the good." To be conceived in sin means to be conceived in mortality, with a fallen nature. It does not mean we are conceived guilty, but the constant enticement of the carnal nature does make sin inevitable in our lives.

To summarize then, the bad news is that without the atonement of Christ we are, by our own premortal choice, trapped in an existence that includes pain, suffering, and anguish. Led by the understandable preference of our carnal natures for pleasure rather than pain, we have fallen into bondage to Satan through personal sin. Our ability to reason is, by celestial standards, impaired, and in its fallen condition serves not our spirits but our flesh. Our emotions are often out of control, and we often think that wrong is right. We are eventually and unavoidably going to die, and when we die, we can't go home. That— without the gospel—is the bad news of the Fall. But don't get depressed; the good news is that the Fall and all its effects have been overcome by Jesus Christ, and they will be removed from us when this mortal test is over.

WHY WOULD WE CHOOSE TO FACE THIS?

If the Fall brought about the conditions listed above, then why would beings like you and me agree to experience it? I believe that our premortal willingness to risk the hazards of the Fall was in most cases an act of faith in Christ. We entered the trap of mortality on the strength of God's promise, God's Word, that he would bring us out again if we would repent when we sinned and turn to him, and all but a very few of us spirit children who come into mortality fully intended back then to repent and to turn to him in this life. Thus to become mortal was to put ourselves completely in the Savior's hands, to jump into a pit of alligators and trust him to pull us out. We trusted him that much then, and we covenanted with him that we would experience the Fall and repent and turn to him, if he would overcome all our enemies and provide atonement and resurrection for us. Should he fail, we were doomed, but it speaks highly of our premortal opinion of Christ that we were willing to take that risk. As it turned out, he did not fail to keep that covenant, but many of *us* have. The Savior didn't fail his grand commission, and all we have to do is trust him here and now as much as we did when we voted for him back then—and once again put ourselves completely in his hands.

THE GOOD NEWS: THE ATONEMENT OF CHRIST

Since I have written at length on the Good News in my earlier book, I am not going to rehearse all of that here except to say that Christ has overcome all things and defeated every enemy.

However, if we *choose* to indulge and obey the carnal self, if we seek to please the flesh, if we cherish and nurture the carnal thought rather than cast it out of our minds, if we obey our inappropriate emotional impulses, or if we continue to insist that wrong is right after the Spirit or inspired leaders instruct us otherwise—then we are accountable for those personal choices. In those cases, our fallen nature has merely tapped on the door, but we have yanked it open and eagerly embraced what was on the other side instead of keeping the door shut. In those cases we are not merely struggling with a fallen nature that keeps whining its preferences at us; rather we have crossed the line and committed willful, personal sin. And for that we will be held accountable unless we repent.

Part of the Good News of the gospel is that the physical, spiritual, mental, emotional, and moral aspects of the Fall have all been overcome by the Savior, and we will eventually be freed from all of them through his grace. Nevertheless, as part of our mortal "test" or probation, we are still required to work under those handicaps until a later time. Disease and death will eventually claim us, no matter how much faith we have. Carnal thoughts will sometimes come into our minds (even, perhaps, in holy places) no matter how righteous we may be. We will make mental errors no matter how converted we are to Christ. Our emotions will inappropriately urge us, and wrong will sometimes seem right no matter how committed we are to the Church and kingdom. We have the promise that the limitations will be removed from us entirely in the resurrection, and that we will not be punished for having suffered them in mortality (unless we *chose* to embrace and obey them), but until that great day we must suffer the frustrations and limitations of wrestling the leering beast. It is part of our test. Our task is to admit our handicap, something some of us find very difficult to do, and yet still to serve as humbly and faithfully as we can until it is removed. Moreover, as we learn to obey God's commandments and progress in becoming more and more like him, we will find that the influence of the carnal self in our lives diminishes over time.

I know people in the Church who beat themselves up for having fallen natures, who take it as a sign that they are not worthy of the kingdom. For these spiritual masochists it isn't enough to *control* their carnal nature or to begin diminishing its influence by developing habitual obedience to God—they don't even want to *have* a carnal nature. They foolishly expect their conversion to the gospel and their desire to lead celestial lives to overcome all the effects of the Fall right now—but it won't happen. The "mighty change" is a change of orientation, desire, and goals that allows us to receive the blessings of the Atonement. But most of us will not achieve all our spiritual goals in this life. It is a process that will continue into eternity. In mortality, *resisting* the urges of our carnal thoughts and putting them out of our minds is a reasonable goal and expectation. But not ever *having* a carnal thought is an unreasonable goal and expectation. President Brigham Young put it this way: "Do not suppose that we shall ever in the flesh be free from temptations to sin. Some suppose that they can in the flesh be sanctified body and spirit and become so pure that they will never again feel the effects of the power of the adversary of truth. Were it possible for a person to attain to this degree of perfection in the flesh, he could not die neither remain in a world where sin predominates. . . . I think we should more or less feel the effects of sin so long as we live, and finally have to pass the ordeals of death."[9]

---

[9]*Journal of Discourses* 10:173.

Now, the preceding paragraphs tell the truth, but there is great danger in saying those things. The danger is that someone, somewhere, is going to think that *resisting* their carnal nature is impossible. That is not correct; resistance is not only possible, it is required. In this life progress is possible—perfection is not.[10] What is impossible is being totally separated from our carnal self. We are stuck, like missionaries with companions who won't get out of bed. We can't just leave them. So we do the best we can to keep the rules ourselves while trying to make the companionship as productive as possible under the circumstances. And we look forward to a transfer. So in the flesh we do the best we can to resist the influence of our carnal companion and to keep the rules while trying to make our lives as productive as possible under the circumstances. And we look forward to the resurrection.

The effects of the Fall (physical, spiritual, mental, emotional, moral) constitute external handicaps that we must all work under in mortality, but we are promised that they will be removed from us in eternity through the victory of Christ. The compulsive and the perfectionists among us need to realize that a large part of why things go wrong in this life is the Fall—not their own incompetence. Once we understand and accept the natural limitations placed upon us by the Fall and its consequences,

---

[10]Granted that since Christ achieved it, perfection must be a *logical* possibility, but since none of the other hundred billion of us has, I argue that it is a *practical* impossibility and an unreasonable goal or expectation apart from Christ.

then we must come to grips with the more dangerous internal hazards that face us in our attempt to follow Christ—our own sins.

Chapter Four

FAITH AND WORKS

Among other things, I hope the first three chapters of this book have established at least the following:

1. As members of the Church in good faith who have entered the gospel covenant, we are *already* in the kingdom of God (though only conditionally at present) for as long as we choose to remain.

2. Enduring faithfully to the end does not just mean "coping" successfully with our problems or suffering affliction with stamina, although some have been called upon to do these things in order to endure. Certainly it has little to do with overcoming personal obstacles or achieving personal goals. Rather it means *staying put* in the kingdom by holding on to Christ and to his church without altering our commitment—no matter what. Neither "enduring" nor "being faithful" means being perfect or living from our baptism until our death without sinning, for God has anticipated our weaknesses and has

prepared the sacrament as a means of ongoing repentance and improvement *within* the covenant.[1]

3. Some of the imperfections that so bedevil us in mortality are not of our own choosing, and we will not be held accountable for them. Imperfections of this type are built-in handicaps and limitations that simply come, because of the Fall, with mortality, and when we put off mortality we shall put off these handicaps as well.

THEN WHY WORK?

Now if all the above are true, then why should I work anymore? After all, if we are already in the kingdom, then the purpose of doing good works cannot be to get into the kingdom! The works must fit in differently somehow, for we can't be working to earn something we already possess. But if the monumental task before me as a mortal member of the Church is *not* to work my way into the kingdom, then what is it? If I'm already in the kingdom, why am I working so hard? In fact, why should I work at all?

Some Christians have no good answers to those questions, since they do not possess the fullness of the gospel plan. They see salvation as a single event, in fact the only really significant event there is, and for them once you reach the kingdom the ball game is over and won. But for

---

[1]Of course, some sins are serious enough to threaten the covenant relationship itself. These must be discussed with the Lord's representative, the bishop or branch president.

Latter-day Saints the answer is not that simple. We see the saving work of God in its entirety, not as a single event but as a *process* with a beginning and an end. The beginning of the process is coming to Christ through faith, repentance, baptism, and receiving the Holy Ghost. In doing so, and at any point in the process thereafter, we are justified, sanctified, and "saved" on the condition of endurance (Matthew 10:22), that the process continue. Thus far, LDS theology is similar to that of other Christians. But Latter-day Saints know that the end of the process is far, far grander than even this. The ultimate goal, the purpose for all God's work, is not merely to save us from death and hell, as wonderful as that is in itself. The purpose behind it all is to make us what Christ is. (Is that monumental enough for you?) To be saved is to become sons and daughters of God through the atonement of Christ—but the ultimate goal for sons and daughters is to grow up and be what their parents are. That is the dimension only Latter-day Saints understand! I'm not working now, after my conversion, to get into the kingdom; I'm not working to be "saved"; I'm working to become what he is, and to do what he does, and to have what he has.

One could say that coming to Christ is like getting on a train headed for a specific destination. If you want to go to that place, it is *critically* important to get on the train. And having gotten on the train, if we stay on it, we will inevitably arrive at the destination. But even so, merely getting on the train is not the point of the journey.

Arriving at our destination is the point of the journey. Coming to Christ, being saved, begins our transformation. It gets us on the train, so to speak. But our ultimate object, our goal, is to become what Christ is. And that is why we work, not to save ourselves from hell—Christ has already done that for us. In his great condescension, God the Son became everything we are and suffered everything we suffer in order to remove every obstacle and open every door (Revelation 3:8); now he invites us to become everything he is by treading the path he has cleared. So we work to close the distance, to become more like our Father (Mosiah 5:7), to actualize the individual perfection Christ has made possible. Those who do not desire to become entirely as Christ now is will find themselves increasingly uncomfortable with the process and will eventually get off the train, some nearer and some farther from their proper destination.[2] But nobody gets *thrown* off. If we stay on board—if we endure to the end—we have God's promise that we shall reach our destination and become all that he is and receive all that he has (Romans 8:14–19, especially 17; John 16:15; Luke 12:44; D&C 84:38).

Unfortunately that is the answer other denominations cannot use, for in their theology we and Christ are usually different species of beings—he is divine and we are human. In their view, it is blasphemous to suggest we can

---

[2]It is possible to be saved in a kingdom of glory, even in the celestial kingdom, without fully becoming what God is (D&C 131:1–4; 132:17).

become what he is. They would insist there is no process, no long-term goal, and no point to religion beyond the single event of being saved from death and hell. Once saved, they are left theologically with nowhere to go, nothing to do, and no reason to do it. Their train is stationary—no engine, no tracks, no journey. For them getting on the train *is* the complete destination. No wonder the one-time event of "being saved" becomes for them the focal point for all eternity and the LDS insistence on working toward a further goal irritates them so—they deny the existence of any further goal beyond merely being saved from death and hell. They mistakenly suppose the Latter-day Saints are working to be saved, and, unfortunately, so do some of our own people. But Christ has already done that work; now we work to become as much like him as we desire to.

Only the Latter-day Saints understand that the purpose of God's grace is to take us all the way to himself and make us—quite literally—what he is. Now that is grace indeed! For Latter-day Saints the focal point of *this* life must be coming to Christ and beginning the process, but we also look forward to that greater moment in eternity when we shall finally be like him (1 John 3:2; 2 Corinthians 3:18). And toward that glorious day as faithful sons and daughters we consecrate ourselves in the everyday unfolding of our lives, that by our labors we might close the gap between us. When we use the term *coming to Christ* in describing conversion, it is a figure of speech that describes our intent and our desires. But the ultimate realization of coming to Christ is in actually closing the distance between us by becoming what he is through doing what he does.

If we focus too much attention on the beginning of life in Christ, on our initial conversion and justification by faith in Christ (that is, on being saved), it is possible to obscure the object, goal, and purpose of our new life, which is gradually, both now and in the eternity before us, to become in actual fact like Christ. Too much emphasis on beginning obscures the importance of finishing. As absolutely essential as it is to be converted, if we do not then begin to imitate Christ and move gradually toward him, we do not really honor him or truly worship him, for true worship is imitation.

Similarly, if we focus too much attention on the final accomplishment of our eternal goal, on becoming someday what our Father is, it is possible to undervalue or even overlook Christ's saving work, to glorify our own efforts instead and feel we are "saving ourselves" by working toward our goal. For that reason many miss the full power and blessing of having Christ in their lives right now. Thus, I suggest it is better to think of salvation as a process with a beginning in this life and an end in eternity.[3] The beginning is mostly up to Christ; the end is mostly up to us. That is what Nephi tells us in 2 Nephi

---

[3]Protestants, however, would use the term *salvation* only for the beginning of the process—not believing there is an end. If we adjust definitions appropriately, we are actually talking about the same thing.

31:19–20: We got into the strait and narrow path by unshaken faith in the word of Christ, relying wholly upon the merits of him who is mighty to save. Now we must press forward with a steadfastness in Christ and a perfect brightness of hope. If we "endure to the end" in this fashion, the Father promises, "Ye shall have eternal life." But we must always remember that while we are genuinely engaged in this process, while we labor between its beginning and its end, we are safe in his kingdom and in his loving arms—*saved* in the classical sense (Alma 5:33, 34:16; Mormon 5:11, 6:17).

OTHER REASONS TO WORK

There are also other reasons to do the work of the kingdom. First, our work for the kingdom is a form of worship; in fact, it is the highest form of worship. God, in all his glorious attributes, in all his perfect righteousness, is our God. We love and respect and seek what he is. How can we worship him and not worship what he *is?* We can't, for that would be a logical contradiction. A thing is what it is; we cannot worship a thing and not worship what it is. Therefore we honor, respect, and value righteousness—for he is righteous. We value love— for he is love. We value compassion and forgiveness—for he is compassionate and forgiving. And what we value we seek to possess. Thus we worship God by seeking to possess his divine attributes in our own lives. The false gods of wealth, fame, sex, and so on are worshiped by pursuing them and seeking to possess them. The person who worships money seeks to possess money; the person who worships fame seeks to be famous; and so forth. The true God is love, truth, and light. So if we truly worship him, we pursue and seek to possess for ourselves love, truth, and light. We cannot seek good, pursue good, worship good—without *becoming* good (or at least without becoming better over time). The real question we must ask ourselves about eternity is not "What do I want to get?" or even "Where do I want to go?" but rather "Who do I want to be?"

We also work to testify. The scriptures give us several examples of this: "Let your light so shine before men, that they may see your good works, and glorify your Father which is in heaven" (Matthew 5:16). "By this shall all men know that ye are my disciples, if ye have love one to another" (John 13:35). If Christ and I are truly one in the gospel covenant, then I must truly reflect his nature in my life. My behavior, in changing for the better, testifies of the Christ who has taken me to himself. The final result may not appear for some time, but the process of positive change in me will be unmistakable. If his countenance does not become, over time, more and more visible in me, if I do not begin to bear the fruits of my conversion, it becomes doubtful that I have really entered into the covenant in good faith or that I have not secretly changed my mind somewhere along the line.

Moreover, according to Ephesians 2:19–22, we members of the Church are like the individual stones or bricks in the structure of the Church. Now, what exactly do stones *do?* What great works do they perform? Well, they are just *there*; they don't really *do* anything! Maybe that is so . . . but they are *always* there! That, in fact, is what they *do*. They are there. They are reliable; they are stead-fast; they can be counted on—they endure in the place where they've been put. That is how they serve the Master Builder. They don't come and go; they don't move or wander; they don't try to check out for a rest or shift their part of the burden to their neighbors—they don't leave a gap in the wall.

Also, we do good works to build the kingdom itself. In my experience, it is those who are *most* converted to the gospel who work the hardest for the gospel's sake. The truth is that the greatest works *follow* conversion—they do not precede it. Joseph Smith laid down his life, the pioneers crossed the plains, early Christians went to the lions, not so they could become converted to the gospel but *because of* their conversion to the gospel.

Consider the following scriptures:

1. Alma 7:24: "See that ye have faith, hope, and char-ity, and *then* ye will always abound in good works" (emphasis added). Clearly, Alma understands these abounding good works to be a result of our faith, our hope, and our charity. The good works of Alma himself came only after his remarkable conversion to Christ. Alma was positively wicked until he accepted Christ and was redeemed; *then* he "labored without ceasing."[4]

---

[4]See Alma 36:12–24 (especially 24).

2. Ether 12:4: "Whoso believeth in God might with surety hope for a better world, yea, even a place at the right hand of God, which hope cometh of faith, maketh an anchor to the souls of men, which would make them sure and steadfast, *always abounding in good works, being led to glorify God.*" Again, note that people abound in good works *after* receiving their anchor of faith and hope. It is conversion to Christ that convinces us of our need to improve and creates the desire to repent and do good works. Good works are generally the fruit of accepting the gospel covenant rather than vice versa.

3. Moroni 7:28: "He hath answered the ends of the law, and he claimeth all those who have faith in him; and they who have faith in him will cleave unto every good thing." It is our faith in Christ and his claim upon us that compels us as Saints to seek after good. True Saints *will* cleave unto every good thing—not so they may claim him, but because he has claimed them.

Also, I believe there is an indisoluble link between labor and happiness, a law that says something like "You can have only as much joy as you are willing to sweat for." Our eternal nature as children of God may be such that our *capacity* for joy is increased by work (opposition in all things). After all, couch-potatoes miss a lot of happiness in *this* life; perhaps in the eternities spiritual couch-potatoes likewise miss something that might otherwise have been theirs with more effort.

If we want to be like God, we must remember that God *works*; he works very hard. And if God's work and glory are to bring to pass the immortality and eternal life of his children, then to avoid his work is also to miss his glory.

Finally, sons and daughters of the house do the chores of the house. Just as Christ did "the works which the Father hath given" him (John 5:36), so we, in imitating him, also do the chores he has given us: "He that believeth on me, the works that I do shall he do also" (John 14:12). My own son, Michael, doesn't obey me at home and do his chores in order to become my son. I don't say, "Gee, Mike, if you do your chores really well you just might be my boy someday." He is *already* my son, and he knows it; that happened years ago. Conversely, were I to instruct the Karlsven kids across the street to mow my lawn, they probably wouldn't do it, because I'm not their dad, and it's not their lawn. They don't owe me any chores. Michael obeys me *because* he's my son, for the sake of a relationship that already exists, and which he values. He obeys to affirm that he willingly accepts the terms of sonship and his rightful place in our family. Michael cannot with any amount of work, service, or obedience *become* my son because he already *is* my son (though he could by calculated disobedience reject the relationship and damage it to the point that it was a mere biological fact and nothing more). Because both of us treasure the relationship and because we love each other, I try to be an understanding parent and he tries to be an obedient son. In the same spirit and for the same reasons, we sons and daughters of the kingdom do the works our Heavenly Father has given us to do. If we want to continue, to endure, in that glorious relationship, then to the best of our abilities we do our chores.

THE SCRIPTURAL NECESSITY OF WORKS

The scriptures make crystal clear that proper behavior (works) *must* be part of our life in Christ. The Savior himself taught, "Not every one that *saith* unto me, Lord, Lord, shall enter into the kingdom of heaven; but he that *doeth* the will of my Father which is in heaven. . . . Depart from me, ye that *work* iniquity" (Matthew 7:21, 23; emphasis added). In other words, merely acknowledging Jesus' lordship, merely saying the words or making the confession, while refusing to make him *our* lord by serving him and conforming our behavior to his will— this will not get us into the kingdom. The confession or the acknowledgment must be accompanied by *doing* the will of the Father in heaven and by *not* doing iniquity. Jesus explicitly established the undeniable link between salvation and good works: "If thou wilt enter into life, keep the commandments" (Matthew 19:17). In John's Gospel (3:20–21) he is quoted as saying: "Every one that doeth evil hateth the light, neither cometh to the light, lest his deeds should be reproved. But he that *doeth* truth cometh to the light, that his deeds may be made manifest, that they are wrought in God" (emphasis added). You can't *do* evil and be in the light—our deeds and our spiritual condition and destiny are interconnected. Moreover, Jesus also makes keeping his commandments—that is, behavior—a part of abiding in his love: "If ye keep my commandments, ye shall abide in my love; even as I have kept my Father's commandments, and abide in his love" (John 15:10; see also 14:15, 21). The necessary link between proper behavior and being "in Christ" is further taught by John: "He that saith, I know him, and keepeth not his commandments, is a liar, and the truth is not in him. But whoso keepeth his word, in him verily is the love of God perfected: hereby know we that we are in him" (1 John 2:4). Who is truly "in Christ"? Those who keep the commandments![5] There are those who profess him but will not *work* for him, those who claim to be sons and daughters but refuse to do their chores. But these, according to the scripture, are "liars."

The necessity of good behavior for abiding in Christ is again emphasized by John at 1 John 3:6–8: "Whosoever abideth in him sinneth not: whosoever sinneth[6] hath not seen him, neither known him. Little children, let no man deceive you: he that *doeth* righteousness is righteous, even as he is righteous. He that committeth sin is of the devil; for the devil sinneth from the beginning" (emphasis added).

Finally, the Apostle Paul, who cannot be accused of

---

[5]Though, as I make clear in *Believing Christ*, "keeping the commandments" is not the same as "*always* keeping *every* commandment." There is room in the covenant relationship for our errors and weaknesses (though not for rebellion) as long as we are improving.

[6]The Joseph Smith Translation clarifies that John is not referring to the occasional infraction but to willful and repeated sinning by reading "*continueth* in sin" here (emphasis added).

being anti-grace, teaches the necessary connection between salvation and good works in several places, among them 1 Corinthians 6:9–10: "Know ye not that the unrighteous shall not inherit the kingdom of God? Be not deceived: neither fornicators, nor idolaters, nor adulterers, nor effeminate, nor abusers of themselves with mankind, nor thieves, nor covetous, nor drunkards, nor revilers, nor extortioners, shall inherit the kingdom of God." Period. No exceptions—not even for *Christian* adulterers, *Christian* thieves, or *Christian* extortioners. In the jargon of my students, God will not accept our talking the talk without our walking the walk.

FAITH AND WORKS

Now, the doctrine of justification by faith is thoroughly scriptural (see, for example, Galatians 2:16; 2 Nephi 2:5; D&C 20:30), but the doctrine of justification by faith *alone*, without any effort, obedience, commitment, or response on the part of the believer, is not.[7]

Some Christians (but not as many as you might think) argue that God requires nothing of us after our conversion, but that he will lovingly accept any lifestyle the saved may subsequently choose to wallow in—thus subsidizing their sins like a rich, indulgent, or gullible parent who keeps paying the bills for spoiled, ungrateful, and

---

[7]The phrase *by grace alone* does not occur in the Bible. The phrase *by faith only* is found at James 2:24 but in a passage that explicitly *denies* justification is possible in this way.

rebellious children. To Latter-day Saints, such a view insults the dignity, justice, and righteousness of God.

On the other hand, for many years "popular" Mormonism (that counterfeit religion invented by members stuck for an answer) has wrongly promoted the other side of the false dilemma of grace versus works. Because the "enemy" (that is, the Baptists, Pentecostals, or whomever they are arguing with) dismiss the need for works and exalt grace alone, it has been felt for some inexplicable reason that *we* must take the opposite position, dismissing grace and exalting works alone. The resulting "popular" theology is just as defective as the adversarial attitude toward other Christians that goes along with it.

Since the scriptures—not just the Bible but *all* the scriptures—discuss the importance of *both* grace *and* works, we are not at liberty to choose sides or to throw out one in favor of the other. Any theological view that slights the vital role of either grace or works is defective. Luther was wrong to ignore James. Latter-day Saints are wrong to shy away from Paul. Both James and Paul wrote the word of God. Both the Epistle of James and the Epistle to the Romans are scripture. Unfortunately, some LDS missionaries, when confronted with Paul's "By grace are ye saved" (Ephesians 2:8) or "A man is justified by faith without the deeds of the law" (Romans 3:28) have counterattacked with James' "Faith without works is dead" (James 2:26) as though Paul was *wrong* or as though James somehow cancels out Paul.[8] But

---

[8] I was guilty of this myself as a missionary, though it wasn't a part

Paul was an apostle of the Lord, and his letters are just as much the word of God as the letter from James (see the eighth Article of Faith). We cannot choose sides between grace and works—*both* must be right!

THE COVENANT

The larger theological perspective needed to accommodate both grace and works is provided by the scriptures themselves in the concept of "covenant," an agreement entered into voluntarily by two parties, with obligations laid upon both. This concept is taught in both the Old and New Testaments as characterizing the proper relationship between God and his people.[9]

The availability of the covenant, the Savior who mediates it, his agony that empowered it—these are all free gifts of grace: God didn't have to offer; Jesus didn't have to suffer. They are gifts bestowed upon us out of love. But the decision to remain in the covenant, to stay

---

of the authorized missionary discussions. I learned it from my senior companions and taught it to my junior companions. For all I know, green missionaries are still getting the infection (the idea that James was right and Paul was wrong) in this manner and passing it on to others.

[9]See, for example, Genesis 6:18 (Noah), Genesis 15:18 and 17:2 (Abraham), Exodus 34:27–28 (Moses), 2 Samuel 23:5 (David), 2 Kings 11:17 (Jehoiada), 2 Kings 23:3 (Josiah), and many others in the Old Testament. The relationship brought about by Jesus is a *new* covenant according to the New Testament. See Hebrews 8:7–13; 9:15–20 (where "testament" means "covenant," as the JST notes). In fact, the Greek word translated "testament" is also the word for *covenant.* The New Testament *is* the new covenant.

put and "endure to the end"—that choice is ours, and it is indicated by whom we serve and by the works we do. As long as we choose to remain loyal to him, Christ continues to justify us by his grace and to atone for our mistakes. Our present good works (such as we can manage) are a *token* of the perfect righteousness we genuinely seek to offer but at this point can achieve only through Christ, a token that we still serve him and not the Enemy. This token—our sincere effort—is accepted by Christ, who alone redeems and justifies us through the covenant.

Ultimately, salvation is the task of him who bears the title—Savior. It is his title because it is *his* function and not ours. Occasionally, he allows us to work for him as tools in saving others, but never for ourselves. We can't baptize ourselves, bless ourselves, ordain ourselves, or endow ourselves. Still, we can and must do something to enter into and remain in the covenant. We cannot logically insist he is our master while at the same time refusing to serve him. We can't have it both ways. Servants, by definition, *serve.* If entering into the covenant is a choice for Christ rather than Satan, then staying in the covenant is serving Christ—that is, to continue choosing Christ, to endure or persist in choosing Christ—and that choice is expressed in our behavior. We can't come to Christ and then just wander off to do our own thing.

Though some find it offensive, it is still true that the relationship alluded to by the biblical terms "servant" and "master" is the institution of slavery. In fact, the term

"redeem" means literally "to buy back." Satan owned us;
we were his slaves, and Christ bought us back. But Jesus
didn't buy us with his own blood so that we could belong
to ourselves—we now belong to him. That's why he is the
Master and we are his servants. And we therefore *owe* him
our service; and we owe *him*—not sin, not the devil, not
ourselves—just him. We are his servants, bought and paid
for with his precious blood (1 Corinthians 6:20).

To say "Christ is Lord" unhypocritically is to say
Christ is *my* Lord. And to say "Christ is my Lord" unhypocritically is to serve him and to reject Satan. Scripture
assures us that we cannot merely assert his lordship without serving him and then hope to enter his kingdom
(Matthew 7:21). You cannot be his servant without serving
him. This is talking the talk without walking the walk.

On the other hand, works without the grace of Christ
cannot save us, for on our best day, due to the limitations
of the Fall, it takes more to keep us going than we can
produce (see Mosiah 2:21; Luke 17:7–10). We can by our
works, by our best efforts, only confirm our loyalty to our
Savior and our desire to continue being justified by his
grace. And our obedience to his commandments, that
imperfect token of our perfect intentions, affirms our
decision to remain in the covenant.

JAMES VERSUS PAUL

Perhaps the greatest scriptural puzzle concerning the
roles of faith and works is presented in the apparently con-
trasting views of James and Paul in the New Testament.

We shouldn't minimize the apparent contradiction. On the one hand Paul says in Romans 3:28, "*A man is justified by faith without the deeds* of the law" (emphasis added). On the other hand, James, the Lord's own half-brother, says in James 2:14 and 24, "What doth it profit, my brethren, though a man say he hath faith, and have not works? can faith save him? [Remember, Paul said yes!] . . . Ye see then how that *by works a man is justified, and not by faith* only" (emphasis added). This apparent contradiction has spawned centuries of heated arguments over whether we are justified by our faith or justified by our works and has caused many students of the scriptures to reject one side in favor of the other. I believe the key to the puzzle may lie in the fact that Paul and James define the word *faith* differently in their writings. James defines faith as most modern readers would—as mere belief. Thus he points out that the devils also believe, and tremble. That is, they believe, but they're still going to be damned—mere belief won't do them any good.

On the other hand, Paul clearly understands faith to be more than just believing. For him *faith* still retains its Old Testament meaning of "faithfulness" (see above, pp. 23–25) or commitment to the gospel. In 1 Timothy 4:1 and 5:8, for example, "the faith" is clearly that to which we are faithful, that is, the gospel covenant, which he further describes as being "kept" or "denied" by good or bad behavior.[10] Twice in his letter to the Romans, at 1:5

---

[10]Most scholars deny that Paul wrote the Pastoral Epistles (1 and 2

(where it is mistranslated in the King James Version) and at 16:26, Paul uses the phrase "the obedience of faith," further indicating that obedience or behavior is a part of faith as he defines the term.

Now, if we use Paul's definition of faith as faithfulness to the gospel covenant, then we find that Paul's formula in Romans 3:28 is correct: Faith alone (commitment to the gospel) *will* justify us to God, even without living the law of Moses. On the other hand, if we define faith as James does—as mere belief—then James' formula is also correct: Mere belief or affirmation without good behavior is insufficient by itself to justify us before God. If we use James' narrow definition of faith, then James' formula is correct. If we use Paul's broader definition of faith, then Paul's formula is also correct. Both apostles teach the truth. Where we get into trouble is in combining James' definitions with Paul's formula or vice versa. Plugging Paul's definition of faith into James' formula would make us say that faithfulness to the gospel is insufficient for salvation. Plugging James' definition into Paul's formula would make us say that merely believing in Jesus will save us even without proper behavior. Both of these hybrids are wrong. So if you are still working to get yourself into the kingdom, won't you finally come in out of

---

Timothy and Titus), insisting that these letters were written by Paul's close associates in his name. I think they are wrong, but it doesn't matter here. Paul's "students" can also offer excellent testimony on how Paul and his associates understood and used this term.

the cold? And if you have come into the kingdom in good faith, won't you do your chores?

WORK OUT YOUR OWN SALVATION

Another frequent objection to the doctrine of grace is made by misapplying Paul's teachings in Philippians 2:12: "My beloved, as ye have always obeyed, not as in my presence only, but now much more in my absence, work out your own salvation with fear and trembling." Those who resist the good news of the gospel and would appoint themselves as Savior in Christ's place say, in effect, "Ah, see? Jesus doesn't save us; he doesn't do the work. We save ourselves; we work out our *own* salvation; therefore we don't need any grace or any mercy; we do it all ourselves—and Philippians 2:12 proves it."

Actually, the phrase "work out your (own) salvation" occurs three times in scripture, and in all three instances the sense is exactly the opposite to the distortion cited in the last paragraph. First of all, in Philippians 2:12, the injunction is to obedience with humility rather than with the pride of the "self-saved," knowing that Jesus, and not us, is Lord (verse 11) and knowing that the ability to achieve what we work for comes only from God and not from ourselves (verse 13). In the Book of Mormon, Moroni enjoins, "Ask the Father in the name of Jesus for what things soever ye shall stand in need" and "Come unto the Lord with all your heart, and work out your own salvation with fear and trembling before him" (Mormon 9:27). But how do we ask God in faith for what we need, and come to Christ, while at the same time denying we have any needs, denying implicitly that we even need Christ, as we attempt to work out our *own* salvation? We can't. What Moroni means is to keep the covenant, to do our part with fear and trembling,[11] and to rely on God for what we lack. To work out our own salvation does not mean to do so independently of Christ and his atone-ment. Rather it means to keep our part of the gospel covenant in humility while relying upon the Lord for everything we need and asking him for it in faith. Alma is even more explicit in this regard (Alma 34:37–38): "I desire . . . that ye should *work out your salvation with fear* before God, and that ye should no more deny the coming of Christ; that ye contend no more against the Holy Ghost, but that ye receive it, and take upon you the name of Christ; that ye *humble yourselves even to the dust,* and worship God, in whatsoever place ye may be in, in spirit and in truth; and *that ye live in thanksgiving daily, for the many mercies* and blessings which he doth bestow upon you" (emphasis added). We cannot "work out our salvation" apart from Christ; we cannot "humble ourselves even to the dust" if in our arrogance we think we can save ourselves without Christ; we cannot "live in

---

[11]In the scriptures *fear and trembling* denotes an attitude of reverence and respect but also of *joy.* The phrase comes originally from the messianic Psalm 2:11: "Serve the Lord with fear [that is, with reverence and respect], and *rejoice* with trembling" (emphasis added). Those who embrace the Son (verse 12) tremble with *joy,* not with fear in the modern sense. That is of profound importance, yet it is exactly opposite to the usual interpretation of "with fear and trembling."

thanksgiving daily for the *many* mercies of God" if we deny we've been shown many mercies. In fact, having faith in the Savior, repenting, entering the covenant, and staying put therein are "all we *can* do" (2 Nephi 25:23).

FRUSTRATION WITH GOD'S MERCIES

Some in the modern Church just seem to have a difficult time acknowledging God's great mercy to his Saints. This has been a failing in other dispensations as well. For example, Alma quotes the ancient Prophet Zenock to his own people (and to us) as follows: "Thou art angry, O Lord, with this people, because they will not understand thy mercies which thou hast bestowed upon them because of thy Son" (Alma 3:16). I believe it is a sin of ingratitude to resist the mercies that have been bestowed upon us because of the Son.

Why is it so difficult for some of us to accept and acknowledge the mercy and grace of God? Much of it boils down to the fear that someone, somewhere, will "get away" with something. First of all, we fear that the guilty can "get away" with their sins without suffering. Since it is merciful, the good news of justification by faith in Christ naturally violates our sense of justice. Also, if people are too confident of their place in God's kingdom, they might try to "get away" with doing less work than we think they should do.

Well, as far as not working hard goes, I suggest that love and gratitude are in the long run better motivators of good works than are fear and anxiety. They are certainly superior to depression and despair. If we feel the Savior's love and know that we are his, our desire to serve him will be greater than if we don't know his love and worry that he might send us to hell. Parents whose children obey only out of fear eventually lose their children, but parents whose children obey out of love gain them forever.

As far as the guilty "getting away" with their sins, my colleague Larry Dahl has offered an illustration worthy of repetition here. A young, unmarried couple he knew had become sexually involved. After some time, an unexpected pregnancy, and no small scandal, they repented, were married civilly, and a year later were sealed in the temple. But some of the local sisters were indignant at how "easily" this pair had gotten off. One sister was overheard to say, "Well, if it's that easy to get away with it, why don't we all just have our fun and then repent when we get caught?"

The mistake this sister makes, as Brother Dahl points out, is in thinking that sin is something desirable and that those who sin and repent somehow enjoy an advantage over those who do not sin. Her reaction was not one of moral superiority—it was the *envy* of a carnal nature positively drooling over the goodies others got to enjoy and *anger* because she couldn't have them too. In short, she was green with envy. In her case, sexual misconduct was something she *wanted* to do but didn't "get" to do, and she felt cheated.

Of course, the correct view is that the righteous who have kept the commandments "get" to live faithfully, "get" to have the companionship of the Spirit, and "get" to become more Christlike, while the poor sinners around us are stuck in the mud until they repent. The recently repentant should envy us our uninterrupted service to the Master rather than us envying their recent bondage to the adversary. The proper perspective is that I "got" to enjoy a relationship with Christ for thirty years, while that poor soul has enjoyed life in Christ only for thirty days. I am way ahead of him or her, not behind. I think I'm behind or at a disadvantage only if my hidden value system puts a higher desirability on wickedness than on righteousness! It's a matter of which you really feel is best—the life of sin or life in Christ. If the former, then letting sinners off the hook bothers you, and you want them to suffer (to balance out all that extra fun and pleasure they had and you didn't). If the latter, then you know that their sinful lifestyle was already its own punishment, and you rejoice with the angels over those who have repented and been redeemed.

WALKING THE TIGHTROPE

The two major hazards of pitting faith against works as though they were competitors are (1) antinomianism and (2) do-it-yourself salvation. *Antinomianism* is the scholars' word for the talk without the walk—the belief that grace removes from us any obligation to do good works or that merely saying "Christ is Lord" will guarantee salvation even for wicked and unfaithful Christians. *Do-it-yourself salvation* is my term for the belief that we save ourselves, that we "work out our own salvation" without grace and without being justified through faith in Christ. Theologically we walk a tightrope between these two equally disagreeable extremes. The finished product of the covenant relationship, neither all grace nor all works, is a faithful Christian saved in the kingdom of God through the grace of Christ. Without the grace of Christ there is no salvation. But without our faithfulness there is no salvation either. Like two blades of the scissors, to borrow C. S. Lewis's analogy, both grace and works must be part of the process. That is why the relationship is described in the scriptures as a *covenant* rather than a gift of grace alone or a reward for works alone. The saved are involved in the salvation process and contribute to it because they are involved in the covenant and must "keep" it. Leave out grace or leave out our own efforts and desire, and you are left with only one half of the scissors—not enough to do the job. Latter-day Saints do not reject the proposition that we are saved by grace. We do, however, reject the proposition that grace can save us against our will or without our consent or while we rebel against Christ.

Still, there is no life so wretched or talent so small or strength so tiny that its consecration will not be accepted for now, that the process of salvation might begin. But our lives must be offered, the consecration must be made, and our proud hearts must break. Thus anyone who desires Christ more than he or she desires sin, from whatever background or with whatever history, may enter into Christ's covenant and be saved.

Chapter Five

HAZARDS TO ENDURANCE

As we attempt to keep our part of the gospel covenant and endure faithfully to the end, there are specific hazards to our individual endurance beyond the limitations of the Fall and our struggle with a carnal nature. In Matthew 24:9–13 the Savior's wonderful promise to those who will endure includes a warning against three specific things to watch out for. These specific hazards are weakness in affliction, deception, and iniquity. Concerning affliction the Lord has said to his disciples: "They [shall] deliver you up to be afflicted, and shall kill you: and ye shall be hated of all nations for my name's sake. And then shall many be offended, and shall betray one another, and shall hate one another" (Matthew 24:9–10).

Satan is an abuser, and one of his first tactics in approaching the faithful is therefore to threaten, bully, and abuse. We have in the Church both historical and contemporary examples of those who couldn't take it and who broke their covenants rather than face opposition, criticism, or unpleasantness. They couldn't bear the malice of the world, and the malice of the world is one of those things we are promised if we are faithful to Christ (John 15:18–19). The world's standard is "You gotta go along to get along." But the gospel standard is uncompromising when it comes to our covenant obligations and our relationship to Christ. These must remain non-negotiable. Still, when Satan has threatened some of the Saints with pain or loss, they've lost sight of who the winner will be in the cosmic struggle. Consequently they've waffled, let go of their covenants, and given up the kingdom.

On the other hand, Church history provides no better examples of people enduring afflictions faithfully than those of the early pioneers. But as we think of the pioneers and their afflictions, we need to reconsider for a minute what it means to "endure" in circumstances like theirs. Although we naturally tend to think of the living, struggling Saints moving victoriously into the Salt Lake Valley as having "endured" the hardships of the trek West, we must remember that for many of the faithful Saints "enduring to the end" simply meant dying on the way. The old, the young, the sick, the unlucky—they did not endure the hardships of the crossing. Their hardships killed them—by the scores and by the hundreds. Some barely made it out of Nauvoo before they died. Nevertheless, in the gospel sense those who died the first day of the trek "endured to the end" just as much as those who lived to enter the valley. They "endured" because they were faithful to their covenants to the end of their lives. As proud as we may be of the pioneers who overcame the wilderness, we must remember that *enduring* doesn't necessarily mean "winning" or "overcoming." We can't let the marvelous physical endurance of the strong-who-live eclipse the equally marvelous spiritual endurance of the frail-who-die, for the weak and the helpless can endure to the end in the gospel sense as well as the strong.

When I was working on my master's degree at Brigham Young University, I shared several classes with a convert from Finland named Helvi Temiseva. Helvi had contracted polio at eight years of age, and this was followed soon thereafter by rheumatoid arthritis. So from her childhood Helvi had been totally incapacitated. She could not move her neck or her body. She had only partial use of her hands. She came to class in a strange conveyance that seemed a cross between a wheelchair and a bed. Helvi could type a single character at a time or turn the pages of a book (or scratch her nose) with the aid of a long knitting needle that she held in one hand. Only years later did I learn that it took forty-five painful minutes every morning for Helvi to be slowly raised from a reclining to a semi-sitting position so that she could begin her day, and another forty-five painful minutes to reverse the process in the evening so she could sleep.

And Helvi Temiseva never overcame life's obstacles; she never achieved her most cherished goals. She never walked. She never married. She never even defeated her need for twenty-four-hour care. But she endured to the end and was a blessing to all who knew her. When she died at age fifty-two, Saints on two continents mourned her passing. For Helvi radiated the light of Christ; she had as strong a hold on the iron rod as anyone I've known. In her presence, one could not be rude or coarse, could not swear, could not murmur or complain. She never said anything reproachful to me, but her example made me ashamed of all my sins. Helvi uplifted and improved all who met her, but it wasn't her courage that inspired us, it wasn't her victory over life's obstacles, it wasn't even her suffering—it was her commitment to the Savior, how she loved and how she served him even in her weakness, and even when he flatly, utterly denied her most fervent prayers. No, enduring isn't always overcoming. Sometimes it's being crushed and ground to powder—with his name on our lips.

I take considerable moral strength from the example of a pioneer named Orson Spencer, a distant relative, who had been called on a mission to England but interrupted his preparations for it to flee Nauvoo with the Saints in February of 1846. However, a month after leaving Nauvoo, his wife, Catherine, died, so he returned to the city from Iowa to bury her beside the infant they had lost six months earlier. When he finally rejoined his children at Winter Quarters, he was asked by the Brethren there to return East once again to begin the mission to which he had previously been called. In order to accept this call, Brother Spencer had to leave his six children alone and parentless at Winter Quarters. The eldest child, Ellen, was fourteen.

Conditions at Winter Quarters became worse than anyone could have anticipated, and the Spencer children, though tended at times by kindly neighbors, very nearly starved. Later that year, Wilford Woodruff wrote an apology to Brother Spencer, explaining that with so many dying it had been impossible to do more for the Spencer children. After three long years, Orson Spencer was finally reunited with his children in Salt Lake City but had been with them scarcely a year when he was called away from them again—on yet another mission. In his letters to his children, Brother Spencer often wrote, "Trust in the Lord, though he slay you."

I cannot help but think that by modern standards the Spencers would qualify as a "dysfunctional family." But this they put behind them for the gospel's sake. Among the children of Orson and Catherine Spencer were Aurelia Spencer Rogers, the founder of the Primary organization of the Church, and Howard Orson Spencer, later the bishop of Orderville. I find it ironic that in the contemporary Church we find those who would claim the same covenant privileges, the same devotion to the gospel as the Spencers and other pioneers, but who won't even accept a calling in the Primary or an assignment at the stake farm! In the resurrection, how will we face those who gave their lives, who lost their homes and fortunes, who buried their loved ones in shallow graves— all for the gospel's sake—if we wither in the face of trivialities and let go of the rod? How shall we who are unwilling to make the smallest sacrifice for Christ expect to share in *his* infinite sacrifice at the last day? To follow Christ is to follow *him* and not someone or something else. If we love someone or something else more than we love him, we are unfaithful spouses, and our relationship is no longer a marriage.

Some of the greatest trials and afflictions we will face in the Church are the offenses that are a natural part of human interaction. Many people leave the Church or otherwise fail to endure to the end because they have become offended. They feel wronged by someone or something in the Church, and so they get even by breaking their covenants and divorcing Christ. I have always been amazed that the offended among us somehow think it matters whether their complaints are justified or not. They seem to feel that if they truly have been wronged, then they are somehow justified in letting go of the rod. But the validity of the complaints has never been the issue. "OK," I want to say to them, "let's just assume that you are absolutely, 100 percent right. Let's grant that Bishop X was inept and foolish, or that Sister Y was rude and catty, or that President Z betrayed your trust, or that I was insensitive, or that my wife snubbed you. So what? Investigation will reveal that most of these kinds of hurts are inflicted unintentionally, but let's suppose that in your case it was vicious and premeditated. So . . . so what? What does the Savior command (not suggest or advise but *command*) in cases of intentional, personal affront? To 'turn the other cheek' (Matthew 5:39; 3 Nephi 12:39). If his command to us is to turn the other cheek when the offense is intentional, how much more ought we to 'turn the other cheek' when the affront is *unintentional*! But assuming that your complaint is absolutely valid and correct, assuming that you have been deeply wronged, where do you go from there? Why, you get over it and get on with it. After all, does the Christ who suffered infinite agony for our sakes have the right to ask us to put up with a bonehead or two in the Church for his sake? I will wager so. Christ died for the boneheads too, you know. And breaking your covenants with Christ because you dislike someone in the Church is like divorcing a faithful spouse because you can't stand his or her family."

DECEPTION

Although significant individual cases of religious persecution still occur and many Saints bear heavy physical burdens, it does not appear that the mainstream of the LDS Church now has to suffer physical affliction and persecution as it once did for the gospel's sake. In the contemporary Church our biggest collective tests seem now to lie in other areas.

The Savior warned of a second hazard to endurance, perhaps even more relevant to today's Saints than the hazard of weakness in affliction. That is the hazard of deception: "Many false prophets shall rise, and shall deceive many." "For in those days there shall also arise false Christs, and false prophets, and shall show great signs and wonders, insomuch, that, if possible, they shall deceive the very elect, who are the elect according to the covenant" (Matthew 24:11; Joseph Smith–Matthew 1:22).

If Satan can't intimidate or bully us with physical trials, he'll often try to fool us with substitute issues and programs. He would like us to invest our time, talents, and energy in causes that are not the cause of Zion, in the hope they may ultimately replace our commitment to the gospel. Often these other concerns are valid and worthwhile. That is irrelevant. The deception comes in giving these concerns a higher priority in our lives than our gospel covenants and thus to prove unfaithful to our first love, who is Christ. Those who are fooled in this way usually feel the Church is not doing enough in the area of their pet concerns. They may become disenchanted with the program of the Church and begin to follow "alternate voices." These members do not lack zeal; indeed, they are often strong enough to endure tremendous trials. But Satan has diverted their zeal to the defense of other causes instead of Zion, and they don't perceive that their shifting loyalty is really unfaithfulness. Those so deceived do not generally reject Christ; they just decide to interpret his will differently or to serve him in different ways or according to new standards and values, and their original commitments take a backseat to their new agenda. In essence, they change their spiritual compass headings. But the truth is that they couldn't be trusted to hold their original course and keep their original commitments. They didn't endure.

Again and again the Lord has warned the Church about following other voices, as, for example, at D&C 43:5: "This shall be a *law* unto you, that ye *receive not* the teachings of any that shall come before you as revelations or commandments; and this I give unto you that you may *not* be deceived, that you may know *they are not of me*" (emphasis added).

This verse of scripture deserves much more attention than it gets. This is a *law*, a *commandment* from God every bit as binding on the members as "Thou shalt not kill" and "Thou shalt not steal," maybe even more so since it was given specifically to the Church in these latter days. If we are to avoid deception, we are *commanded* by God not to listen to anyone who purports to reveal his doctrine or his will other than the properly called, sustained, and ordained priesthood leadership. Period. No ifs, ands, or buts—no exceptions. This includes religion teachers,[1] authors, neighbors, rumors, newspapers, television, so-called "intellectuals," prevailing scientific

---

[1]As a religion teacher myself, I understand that my calling—like that of many others in the Church—is to "preach, teach, expound and exhort" what has *already* been revealed to the Church. I may occasionally be forgiven for expressing my *opinions*, I suppose, as long as I clearly label them as such and as having therefore no authority. But any *new* information or *additional* revelation whether for all the Saints, for my nine o'clock class, or for my next-door neighbor, cannot come through me. It will come, must come, through the proper channels.

opinion, returned missionaries, brothers-in-law, business partners, housewives, boyfriends, girlfriends, political candidates, a "friend of a friend," a "guy in my ward," mystics, gurus, and "real spiritual people." (Have I left anyone out?) Do we get the message here? Nobody talks for God but God and those properly called by God and properly sustained by the Church to represent him and conduct his business here on earth. I find the blind, ignorant compulsion of so many of the Saints to break this commandment and follow this guru or that self-appointed teacher as scandalous and inexplicable as the compulsion of ancient Israel to worship idols in the groves and high places of the Canaanites. Certainly the stupidity required and the results obtained are the same in both cases.

I don't understand why so many contemporary Saints have difficulty with this principle. God reveals his will to those whose stewardship it is to receive it—individuals for themselves (and *only* themselves), parents for children, bishops for wards, stake presidents for stakes, and so on. However, God reveals *new* doctrine or otherwise speaks to the whole Church in only one way—through revelation to the president of the Church.[2] Why do so many with itching ears (frequently those who most pride themselves on their spiritual maturity) lust so greatly for other channels of spiritual information? I do not know,

---

[2]Should the president be incapacitated, the Lord will continue to lead the Church through the united voice of the prophets, seers, and revelators who are his counselors.

but I have in the past advised more than one of my students to write "D&C 43:5" on their foreheads with a felt-tip marker—and to keep it there until they learn to keep the commandment found therein.

But doesn't God reveal things to people who are *not* priesthood leaders? Isn't it possible for exceptional individuals to learn by direct revelation mysteries that are unknown to others? Yes, this is possible, but always with one *hugely* important condition that is stated in Alma 12:9: "It is given unto many to know the mysteries of God; nevertheless they are laid under a *strict command* that they shall *not impart* only according to the portion of his word which he doth grant unto the children of men, according to the heed and diligence which they give unto him" (emphasis added). In other words, many of the faithful may receive revelations from God—even revelation regarding the mysteries. But they are commanded at the same time to keep their mouths shut! They can share with others what God has *already* revealed to the Church in the scriptures and through his prophets, but the rest is private, and keeping it private is a sacred obligation. In effect the Lord tells those who are blessed with additional insights, "If I wanted everyone to know, I would instruct the prophet to teach it to the Church. But this is for you alone, so keep it to yourself." Therefore, anyone in the Church (or out of it, for that matter) who shares a private revelation out of stewardship does so in violation of God's "strict command." So, for example, if somebody had a vision or an out-of-body experience and then set about instructing the Saints on the nature of the spirit world or the events of the Second Coming, that would be, in my opinion, in direct contradiction to the principle of Alma 12:9 and a betrayal of the Lord's "strict command." This happened once in Joseph Smith's day when an otherwise faithful Hiram Page began "revealing" things to the other members. The Lord instructed the Church at that time that "no one shall be appointed to receive commandments and revelations in this church excepting my servant Joseph Smith, Jun., . . . For I have given him the keys of the mysteries, and the revelations which are sealed, until I shall appoint unto them another in his stead" (D&C 28:2, 7). Hiram Page was well-intentioned, but he was deceived and in time would have deceived others with his false revelations.

Of course, if the Lord does want certain information revealed to the Church, he will, as D&C 28:2 and 43:5 indicate, reveal it through his prophet. There is no room in the doctrinal framework of the Church for freelance revelations or freelance revelators. There are no "independent" religious authorities in the Church and never have been. That is not the way the Lord works. Even if the reported experiences are valid, and they sometimes are, sharing them publicly would be a betrayal of God's confidence. And I frankly have trouble believing that someone mature enough to receive a "special" revelation would then be wicked or foolish enough to turn right around and spill the beans. Maybe if more of us could be trusted to keep our mouths shut, in accordance with

Alma 12:9, we'd get more personal revelation for our own edification! So the bottom line is: when someone inflicts their revelations on others out of stewardship, either they are lying or they are unfaithful—one or the other. Given Alma 12:9 and D&C 43:5, there are no other possibilities, and wise Saints will avoid such revelations and such revelators as the spiritual snares they are.

I encounter another form of this snare almost every year at BYU. I am regularly approached by some student (male or female, though the majority are female) with the following story: "Brother Robinson, my boyfriend (or girlfriend, as the case may be) is a returned missionary, and he has had a revelation that I am supposed to marry him. I'm not really in love with this person, but should I marry him anyway? I don't want to disobey the Lord."

"Well," I reply, "what is the order of the priesthood? Who is entitled to receive revelation for you? The apostles and prophets in the faithful performance of their stewardships. Your stake president, your bishop, your parents, and your husband (also in the faithful performance of their rightful stewardships). Finally, and most importantly, you. You are entitled to receive revelation for yourself, and you are *required* to confirm for yourself all revelation received for you by those in the priesthood line of authority. Is this person, this returned missionary with the revelation, in your priesthood line of authority? No, of course not, though he desperately *wants* to be. Has the Lord confirmed this revelation to you personally? No, he hasn't. Then get as far away from this person as you can, and do it as fast as you can. This is someone who is trying to use your religion to manipulate and control you. Get away now before you are caught in the snare!"

Now, there may be cases from time to time where the Lord reveals to someone whom they are going to marry. My grandmother, Willmia Brown, for example, once heard an audible voice identify Joseph E. Robinson as her future husband, and it turned out to be so. But in such cases the revelation will be kept confidential until the other party has come to the same conclusion. Such a sacred insight will not be used like a crowbar to try to pry someone else into compliance. If it is genuine, it will come to pass on its own.

The Saints need to become more sophisticated in detecting spiritual snake-oil dealers. Whether they're peddling marriage or plural marriage or revelations or books or politics or special doctrines or special diets or herbs and vitamins or the "original" Greek (or Hebrew) or financial advice or "LDS" investments or whatever—if they are using religion to help sell their product or point of view, then they represent the cunning snares of Satan.

REVELATION BY RUMOR?

For me, one of Elder Delbert L. Stapley's most memorable observations, and one of my favorite quotations from general authorities, was "The Saints are suckers." Many of the Saints are indeed suckers, and one way in which this is certainly true involves the Saints' stupid acceptance of rumors. God doesn't govern his church by rumor, and yet some Saints whip themselves into a frenzy over rumors heard outside the proper channels of revelation. I once had a student come to me and ask if I thought he and his wife should drop out of school and sell their car in order to get their year's supply of food by the next April conference. "Probably not," I responded. "Getting your year's supply is an important goal, but right now I would judge it more important for you to make whatever financial sacrifice is necessary for you to finish school. Why would you consider dropping out?" I asked. "Well, because of the prophecy," he replied. "You know, the one where President Benson told his family to be sure and get their food storage by April because 'important things are going to happen then.' Several people in my ward have spoken on this prophecy in sacrament meeting just in the past couple of weeks, and my wife and I are frightened because the only way we can afford to get ready by April is to sell our car and drop out of school."

"Ah, my young friend," I said, finally realizing what had happened, "you have been a victim of the goose-pimple gang.[3] These are the creators and purveyors of 'tabloid religion' in the Church, and they judge the truth of an idea by how exciting, thrilling, or sensational it is—

---

[3]I am indebted to my colleague Joseph F. McConkie for the term "goose-pimple gang." It perfectly describes that nut-ball fringe in the Church who invent, and the gullible Saints who repeat, any story that will produce goose pimples in their listeners. Apparently their standard for "inspirational stories" is not "Is it true?" but rather "Does it give me goose bumps?"

you know, the 'Space Aliens Kidnap President Hunter' sort of thing. The actual gospel is much too tame for the goose-pimple gang, so they are constantly inventing and spreading an 'enhanced' version—the 'tabloid gospel.' You need to inoculate yourself against them by learning a fundamental principle: *The Lord does not govern his church by rumor.* There is no such prophecy as the one reported to you, or maybe more correctly put, there are *dozens* of such prophecies—all bogus. Learn the order of the priesthood, my friend, and learn that rumor has no place in it. Then you will be safe from the further deceptions of the goose-pimple gang and their tabloid gospel."

In the past several years, I have kept track of dozens of "faith-promoting rumors" frequently repeated by the goose-pimple gang. Some that I hear quite often are "The Prophet in the Elevator," "Nephites on the Mesa," and "The Benson Family Special." "The Prophet in the Elevator" comes in many different forms, but basically someone is supposed to have bumbled into an elevator with the president of the Church and been specifically warned to get a year's supply, do genealogy, get a temple recommend, or whatever, because the Second Coming, the call to Missouri, a Soviet nuclear attack, or whatever, is going to take place in April or October—by the next general conference. This story first surfaced in the 1950s and has been told in one form or another about presidents McKay, Smith, Lee, Kimball, Benson, and Hunter. I have no doubt that a revised version involving President Hinckley will be in circulation by the time this book is out.

The "Nephites on the Mesa" has also been around for at least thirty years. Supposedly some good members driving to conference are stopped in the desert between Las Vegas and St. George by a man dressed in black. The stranger warns the members to accomplish some spiritual goal (food storage, genealogy, and so on) by a certain date because something apocalyptic is about to happen. The man in black then asks to be let out, and as the car drives away, he vanishes from sight. Obviously, he was one of the Three Nephites. Less obvious is why these instructions for the Church didn't come through the proper channels.

I am privileged to count as a friend and colleague Brother Reed Benson, eldest son of the late President Ezra Taft Benson. After checking out a dozen or so rumors attributed to Reed or to his family over several weeks, it occurred to me to ask him how many such inquiries he actually received. "Oh, it seems like about sixty a week," he replied. "Sometimes I wish they'd let me talk at conference just so I could tell the Saints all at once that the Benson family hasn't had any special revelations, special prophecies, special visitations, special family councils, special ordinations, or special information. The gospel is the same for us as it is for everybody else." Once again— *the Lord does not govern his people by rumor.*

Other fertile sources for rumors are "a friend of a friend's patriarchal blessing" or supposed missionary stories. Patriarchal blessings fall into the category of individual revelation, so if there is special information in a blessing, the commandment of Alma 12:9 to keep it sacred and private would apply. Thus, if it is not *my* patriarchal blessing, any information in it should be deemed unreliable, since if this person were on the up and up, the blessing wouldn't be made public. On the other hand, if it's *my* patriarchal blessing, then the information in it is for me and not for anybody else. Many of the stories one hears about other people's patriarchal blessings, and most missionary stories, have become "urban legends" in the Church and are untrue besides. Stock-in-trade of the goose-pimple gang, they have little power to edify, and they should be ignored by those Saints who are *not* suckers.

MY SHEEP HEAR *MY* VOICE

In the premortal life, all of us rejected Satan and his alternate plans. Now we must do it again. If we are to endure, we must avoid religious "special interest" groups as well as irreligious influences. Not everything labeled "LDS" or that is "religious" is good—there are wolves in sheep's clothing out there. Unfortunately, the wolves have learned that some of the Saints will buy or believe anything, as long as a large "LDS" label is prominently displayed on it. The wolves try to imitate the voice of the shepherd, but *his* sheep listen only to *his* voice and follow only *him* (John 10:27).

Right now there are many other voices, "alternate voices," vying for the attention of the Saints. There are social voices, intellectual voices, political voices, and yet other voices. For example, I have a friend who is now going through a difficult time. He is politically very intense. He is worried particularly about a "new world order" and also about the end of the world. He sees satanic conspiracies all around him, in world events, in the schools, in government, in society, and he can't understand why the Church isn't as intense and as concerned as he is about these threats. He spends a great deal of time trying to "warn" other members of the Church whom he believes to be asleep, and he privately wonders if the Church leadership aren't also asleep. Basically, his thinking runs like this: "My church and my politics are telling me two different things, and I *know* that my politics are true, so there must be something wrong with the Church." He won't consider the other logical possibility—that the Church might be true and his *politics* in need of adjustment. Nor does he recognize his incipient apostasy, the reversal of priorities and loyalty evident in this thinking. He is in danger of making Christ second to his political views—of divorcing his first love. There is often truth in what he says, but that is not the point. The point is that he is listening to other voices and has transferred his *highest* loyalty to programs other than the Lord's. Tragically, his politics have become the idol to which all else in his life must bow—even his commitment to the Church and his covenant with God.[4]

---

[4]I know I will take flack for this paragraph, for many of the faithful Saints [including me] are politically conservative. It is not the politics that are at issue here—it is the priorities. If the Church isn't pursuing a particular path, there are only two possibilities: (1) the Church is wrong, or (2) the path is wrong. Take (2) to the bank.

This shouldn't be a difficult concept for most of us: the Church is true. It's as simple as that. All may not be well in Zion, but the Church is still true. It's not anemic; it doesn't need supplements. It's not true *if,* and it's not true *but,* and it's not true *except.* It's just *true!* Moreover, the Church is not off course; it's not going too slow, and it's not going too fast. Its leaders are not asleep, and they don't need any uninvited help from the passengers to steer the boat. *The Church is true!* Knowing this is what it means to have a testimony of the truth of the restored gospel, and those who maintain otherwise are the deceivers or the deceived who have lost their faith and changed their loyalty and their compass headings, who have divorced Christ for love of an idol, and who have not endured to the end.

MORE OR LESS

Some protection from the hazard of deception may be found in the principle of "more or less": "Truth is knowledge of things as they are, and as they were, and as they are to come; and whatsoever is more or less than this is the spirit of that wicked one who was a liar from the beginning" (D&C 93:24–25; see also 3 Nephi 11:40, 18:13; D&C 10:68, 98:7).

In the context of the gospel, truth is what God has *actually* said, what he *actually* directs, what he *actually* requires—no more and no less. On a straight and narrow path, it doesn't matter whether we fall off to the right or to the left—we are in trouble either way. It doesn't matter whether we are liberals or conservatives, whether we believe too little or too much. If Satan can't get us to abandon the principles of the gospel, he is content that we should live them obsessively or as fanatics. One is less than the will of the Lord; the other is more. Either puts us in the territory of the wicked one.

I know people who won't eat white bread, refined sugar, or chocolate because they believe those things violate the Word of Wisdom. They are obsessed with vitamins, herbs, and supplements. There would be nothing wrong with some of this (they may, in fact, be right in some of their claims), except that they teach it as the will of the Lord and as part of the Word of Wisdom. Their error is in "supplementing" what the Lord has actually revealed with what they *wish* he had revealed—adding to the Word of Wisdom themselves and then calling it the word of God. Satan loves a fanatic as much as a rebel, for they are both off the path and therefore in his power. And there *are* LDS fanatics! One cannot simply assume, because someone is LDS and has a great deal of zeal and a temple recommend, that he or she is therefore correct or even credible. What the Lord has actually said to the apostles and prophets for the Church, or what he has actually said privately to a single individual for that individual (and no one else)—that is the trustworthy standard.

We have in the Church today those who are embarrassed that God has said as much as he has, who find some of his word not to their liking, and who go about trying to discredit the Brethren and neutralize the revelations and commandments. We have others who are embarrassed that God has not said more about their pet concerns, and who go about preaching programs and principles the Lord has never revealed. One takes words out of God's mouth; the other puts them in. Each preaches a "new, improved" gospel inspired by that wicked one who was a liar from the beginning, the very first alternate voice.

It requires discipline to embrace as gospel and to teach as gospel exactly what the Lord has revealed, no more and no less, and to avoid revising the gospel to suit ourselves. But those who can do it will know things as they *really* are (Jacob 4:13) and will avoid deception.

A LIAR FROM THE BEGINNING

Satan lies; it is his essence. As God is truth, and truth is knowledge of things as they really *are,* so Satan is a liar who teaches us things as they *aren't* exactly, but as they *appear* to be and often as we *want* them to be. Satan is the plausible god, the god of appearances, the god of "looks like" and "seems to be." He is the god of things as we wish them to be, and under his influence he lets us create any universe we want—for Satan rules as the god of every false universe so created. In Satan's world any philosophy can be true, any sin can be a virtue, any opinion can be right. The universe can be whatever we want it to be. Because Satan offers us a way of getting what we want, we mortals are vulnerable to his imitation worlds and plausible realities. Of course, the cost is truth, for truth is knowledge of things as they really *are*, not of things as we want them to be. Satan will create a universe to fit any desire, but only God can show us how to fit our desires to the universe—the real universe, the one that won't change to accommodate us. Satan offers a false "truth" to legitimize, or so it seems, our every desire; God would change our desires to fit a single, legitimate truth.

Satan lies. It's such a simple principle, but so few remember it. Instead we blindly assume the truth of rumors, media reports, personal anecdotes, and so forth that reflect badly upon the Church or its leaders. In some future judgment many of the deceived Saints are going to say when they finally learn the truth, "Oh, really? Gee, I wish I'd known that. You see, the information I had was that . . . ," and they will then try to blame their letting go of the iron rod on bad information instead of on themselves for listening to alternate voices. But unfortunately, we will be held accountable for allowing ourselves to be deceived. After all, we have been explicitly forewarned: "Satan will lie so cleverly, even the elect will be at risk."[5] We also have the teachings of the apostles and prophets. We have the counsel of other priesthood leaders. We have the scriptures. We have the gift of the Holy Ghost. We have personal prayer and personal revelation. We have

---

[5]As at Matthew 24:24 or Joseph Smith–Matthew 1:22, here broadly paraphrased.

been given all we need to avoid doctrinal deception, so if we are deceived in doctrine it is unfortunate, but it is usually our own fault. On the other hand, those who take advantage of all these resources, and whose fingers can't be pried off the iron rod, won't be deceived: "Whoso *treasureth* up my word, *shall not be deceived*" (Joseph Smith–Matthew 1:37; emphasis added).

The difficulty is not so much in believing that Satan lies—that is easy enough. The difficulty for many Saints seems to be in believing that Satan could lie skillfully enough to fool even *them* if they let go of the rod. ("Moi, deceived? Oh come now, be serious! The merely *elect* perhaps, but *me?* Never! You see, I'm . . . well, I'm special.") Believing themselves to be "special"—especially intelligent or especially talented or especially intuitive—they insist upon their ability to detect the truth on their own, and then, of course, they are lost. For Satan does lie, and he's very, very good at it. Some Saints are particularly vulnerable to lies told by scholars, others are most vulnerable to lies told by reporters, and still others seem most vulnerable to lies told by friends or social peers. Tragically, with each new lie some of the Saints are fooled and let go of the rod. They don't endure to the end.

Satan is particularly good at lying about people. He slanders the Saints, and the slanders are believable and are believed. One of his scriptural titles, besides "liar from the beginning" (D&C 93:25), is "the accuser of our brethren" (Revelation 12:10). Satan is the archetypical prosecutor or attorney for the plaintiff. He's an accuser, a prosecutor—he never defends. Satan is an inquisitor; he finds fault, and where he finds no actual fault, he cleverly creates the appearance of fault. That is what Satan is; it's what he does; it is his essence to lie and to accuse, and his lying accusations *will often seem correct* to most honest, objective observers. He accused Jesus of blasphemy and treason and got most of the people to believe it. He accused the Lord's Anointed falsely and got away with it. We should not be surprised to see the Brethren in our day, the Lord's anointed in the modern Church, attacked with false accusations in the media of the world. That is what Satan does, what he has done from the beginning.

The promise of the Savior to those that serve him is: "If the world hate you, ye know that it hated me before it hated you. If ye were of the world, the world would love his own: but because ye are not of the world, but I have chosen you out of the world, therefore the world hateth you" (John 15:18–19).

Sometimes we Latter-day Saints get confused on this point. We think that because we are "good," because we are "religious," or because we are pursuing the truth, that the world ought to admire us, and we expect that it will. And we are often surprised to find ourselves despised by the world to the very degree that we really do believe God and try to keep his commandments. We forget whose world this is (at least until the rightful owner comes again to reclaim it). We forget who is presently, for the most part, calling the shots and controlling the perceptions here (2 Corinthians 4:4).[6]

When charges and accusations fly against the Church, when the Brethren are accused, when the world is unanimous in its condemnation, then the faithful need to smell the sulfur and be wary. Of course, there may be real scandals in the Church from time to time—Judas' behavior was certainly a scandal—but usually there are just lies. Given the nature and function of Satan and the past record for honesty of this world that serves him, when charges and accusations are leveled at the Church and its leaders, sons and daughters of the kingdom owe their covenant relationship with Christ at least the benefit of a doubt—and probably the benefit of many doubts. After all, why should the affirmations of a scholar, a reporter, or a disaffected former member be more reliable to me than the solemn affirmations of the Holy Ghost in answer to fervent prayer?

RESISTING THE "CARNAL GRUDGE"

Besides the external opposition of the world to the Saints, there is an *internal* opposition that often goes unrecognized for what it is. The carnal man within us despises our walk by faith. It is an affront and an abomination to him. The carnal self rebels and rages at the sug-

---

[6]Some of us even, instead of helping to build Zion, absurdly and unfairly blame God for the way Satan governs Babylon. You don't like this world? Help build the next one!

gestion that he is morally blind and needs a guide, or that he is not to rule but must be in subjection. The scriptures tell us that the natural man is an enemy to God (Mosiah 3:19), and some of us don't realize that that enemy was not *totally* vanquished at our baptism. The natural self, the carnal man or woman, still resides within us, is still a part of our mortal test—and given its own way is still an enemy to God. Unfortunately, many of us don't recognize this domestic enemy, this sneering would-be traitor within ourselves who responds with immediate and irrational irritation, condescension, or hostility whenever the subject of Zion comes up.

I see these little treasons, for example, in some BYU students who habitually talk about their university or about Utah in a sneering and condescending way. No matter that they may come from cities where you can't safely walk the streets at night, from high schools with the moral standards of a TV series, or from rural areas that are cultural and intellectual wastelands—some still have this sneering disrespect for "Happy Valley" and BYU. Why? Because at some level of their consciousness, they associate these things with the Church and kingdom of God, and the not-yet-completely-vanquished carnal self within them is an enemy to God. Time and again I have seen even faithful members grow hot and hostile or sneering and contemptuous at the suggestion they might subscribe to the Church magazines or support the Church Educational System or read a "Church book." People pretend to themselves that this native resentment of Church culture is rational, but it never is. It is *natural,* and we seldom recognize our resentment for what it is—the natural man or woman sniping from ambush within us at the cause of Zion.

Many otherwise faithful Saints who are trying to follow Christ in most ways nevertheless allow themselves the resentment and irritation of this carnal grudge against some aspect of Christ's kingdom. In every ward there are those with a chip on their shoulder, who are not sinful and wicked or even "inactive," but whose carnal self just resents being subjected to the Spirit, so irritation and resentment become their habitual and normal responses to Church leaders and programs. Their carnal self isn't strong enough to keep them in Egypt, but it does sabotage the wagons all the way to Canaan. If we are obligated to serve God with all our heart, might, mind, and strength and to build his kingdom, can we in good faith resist, resent, or attack any part of that kingdom?

Always the goal of Church programs is to perfect the Saints. Always (so far) they fail to do that completely. That means both the institutional Church and its individual members are trying to do something (achieve perfection) that they fail to do. The carnal self and other critics like to interpret that failure as hypocrisy. "You hypocrites," they say. "You think you're so hot, trying to be so good, but you turn out to be human just like the rest of us." But hypocrisy is having *pretended* values we don't really try to live by, and there is no pretense about LDS values and goals—these are our genuine aspirations.

Moreover, weakness is not the same as hypocrisy, and those who genuinely seek perfection and fall short are no more "hypocrites" than high jumpers or pole vaulters who fail to clear the bar are hypocrites. That is one of Satan's filthy slanders, one that is widely accepted. I have seen people who never even notice the corruptions of Babylon practically foam at the mouth in anger at the imperfection and "hypocrisy" of Church programs. But why should those who aspire to righteousness and fall short be despised more than those who aspire to evil and succeed? Because the natural man is an enemy to God, and the natural man despises any attempt to live by the Spirit.

Now, what makes *you* mad at the Church, its programs or its constituent parts? Think about it. Shall we be double-minded, or single-eyed? Shall we finally decide whose team we're on—and let the consequence follow? Even after we have been converted to the gospel, we must be wary of small treasons against the cause of Zion rooted in the resentment of the carnal self to the control of the Spirit.[7]

Where the natural man has gained even greater control in the life of a person, it no longer snipes from ambush at peripheral programs, but it attacks the central

---

[7] I am not suggesting that faithful Saints can't ever be appropriately critical of Church institutions. But we must recognize and neutralize the grudge our carnal selves may bear them. Many Saints are double-minded in this way. They believe themselves loyal to the kingdom as a whole while being disloyal to its constituent parts.

elements of the Church or attacks the Brethren directly. In cases like these, the carnal self is no longer just resentful; it has become the dominant part of us and attacks the Spirit openly. That is the last step before total loss of the Spirit and complete apostasy.

TWO TYPES OF HYPOCRISY

The Greek word *hypocrites,* usually translated "hypocrite," actually means "actor" or "role-player." A hypocrite in the classical sense is someone who pretends to beliefs and standards that he or she does not really hold or try to live. One may generally encounter more than one type of true hypocrisy in the Church; some of these are malicious and some are not. At least two types of hypocrisy constitute a real hazard to the endurance of faithful Saints: the oxymormons and the role-players.

Type 1: Oxymormons. Most people know what an oxymoron is. It is a term whose component parts deny or contradict each other, like "jumbo shrimp," "criminal innocence," or "true lies." Oxymormons are Church members whose theology does this same thing. Often their true feelings and their stated feelings are not the same, so they end up maintaining mutually contradictory propositions. For example, should someone come along and suggest that we be faithful in a "new" way by rejecting the fundamental propositions of the gospel, then this "unfaithful faithfulness" would be self-contradictory. The desire to *be* unfaithful coupled with the desire not to *appear* unfaithful causes people to talk nonsense. We can't define adultery as a "new" kind of virtue, or abuse as a "new" way of presiding in our homes, or doubting as a "new" way of believing. Neither is darkness a "new" kind of light, or hatred a "new" kind of love. Such claims are moronic as well as oxymoronic. Yet we have in the Church some who would become a "new" kind of Latter-day Saint by denying the definitive tenets of the faith: that Jesus is the Christ, that the Church is true, that Joseph Smith is a prophet, that the Book of Mormon is a true account. These are the oxymormons, and they don't want to leave the Church. They want to *change* it. They want the rest of us to be faithful Saints in a "new" way— by rejecting the faith of the Saints. After all, if all the possible compass headings are labeled "North," then we can never be accused of being off course, no matter where we want to go! A fitting strategy for him who was a liar from the beginning. But this is not being LDS in a "new" way, nor is it enduring to the end. It is unfaithfulness.

Type 2: Role-players. The other type of hypocrisy we encounter from time to time in the Church is the more passive variety I call "role-playing." Most role-players are not malicious; they just want to stay in the Church even though they don't believe in it. But even these casual hypocrites do more damage than they know. For example, several years ago, I bore strong witness to one of my classes that living the gospel could make anyone's home a little bit of heaven on earth. After class one student waited until all the others had gone and then asked me quietly, "Are you lying to us, or are you telling the truth?

Can a family really be that way, or is it all just a fairy tale? I need to know." I asked her why she would ask such a question, and she responded, "My family are all very active in the Church; we are the 'ideal LDS family.' All my life I have watched my parents create and maintain that appearance of faithfulness. Mom is the 'indispensable woman' in our ward, and Dad serves on the high council—but it is all a lie; it's just a role they play until they get home. My brother and I call it 'playing church.' We look like an 'ideal LDS family' on the outside, but on the inside there is nothing. We do not have family prayer or family home evening. My parents neither love nor respect each other, and our home is not heaven. I can't wait to leave and get away from all the contention and hypocrisy. For years I have believed that all LDS families were like mine and that 'living the gospel' meant to everyone else what it means to me—just 'playing church.' I have just assumed that everybody else was playing the same role and creating the same illusion and telling the same lie—and now you are telling me that for some people it's *not* an illusion and *not* a lie?" At that point she began to weep. "I would give anything to have a family like the one you describe, but can it really be like that, or are you just feeding us the same old stuff?" I took her hands in mine and looked her straight in the eye: "I testify to you, on my honor, that I speak the truth. The gospel is true, and its blessings are real to those who will live it. It's not just a comforting fairy tale; it is true."

This young woman had been greatly wounded by role-playing parents, and her ability to believe the promises of the gospel had been impaired as a result. Unfortunately, there are many role-players in the Church, and they usually wound those around them in this same way, though they probably have no intention of doing so. They wound others because they inadvertently teach, nonverbally by their attitudes and their example, that the Church isn't really to be taken seriously, that it's something we just do for social or business reasons, or out of a sense of tradition, or because we think religion is good for the kids, or even because we're just too lazy to break the habits of our youth. Often these role-players know all the right answers and go through all the right motions, but inside they are spiritually dead. Many of them genuinely enjoy being active in the Church, but for the same reasons other people enjoy being active in Rotary or the PTA.

I have known missionaries, students, spouses, and children who have been savaged by the hypocrisy of leaders or parents who were just "playing church" without real testimony or conviction. Such victims come to believe that the Church is just an inside joke that everyone eventually wises up to and then plays along with—like Santa Claus or the Easter Bunny. They are taught this by the lying example of role-players who rob them of the opportunity to genuinely encounter and be led by the Spirit.

If you have been injured or disillusioned by exposure to role-players in the Church, know that the vast majority of members are not such. Endurance requires that we maintain our conviction of the truth even if some others think of the Church as an inside joke. Do not let your testimony or your endurance be diminished by those about whom the Lord has said: "Wo unto them that are deceivers and hypocrites, for, thus saith the Lord, I will bring them to judgment. Behold, verily I say unto you, there are hypocrites among you, who have deceived some, which has given the adversary power; but behold such shall be reclaimed; but the hypocrites shall be detected and shall be cut off, either in life or in death" (D&C 50:6–8).

OTHER HAZARDS:
SPIRITUAL MASOCHISTS AND SADISTS

Spiritual masochists is my term for those who resist the good news of the easy yoke and the light burden (Matthew 11:28–30) and instead imagine such difficult requirements for salvation that they know they cannot possibly make it. Believing that God can't save them puts some people in a state of despair, which, for perverse *carnal* reasons, they prefer instead of joy. Their concern with their own sins and weaknesses is usually obsessive, and it often gives them a certain carnal satisfaction ("*Your* problems and sins are trivial, but *mine* are too complex even for God to resolve!") These individuals need to repent, not (at least not at first) of any single transgression but rather of their wallowing self-indulgence on the one hand and their lack of faith in the infinite power of Christ on the other.

Spiritual sadists are those who want the rest of us, especially those of us who are struggling with problems or afflictions, to know how *difficult* salvation will be for us. I think they are worried that heaven might be too crowded, or perhaps they're worried about having to share it with lesser beings than themselves, so they're trying to cut down on the numbers by doing a little weeding out before they get there. Both spiritual masochists and spiritual sadists operate under the direction of carnal rather than spiritual motives, and both can be a hazard to the endurance of the young, tender, or inexperienced.

I once asked a close friend why she had left the Church as a teenager to return only after many years, and I discovered that she had been deceived by a spiritual sadist. "I remember sitting in my Laurel class," she said, "and the teacher was telling us how good and how pure we had to be to go to the celestial kingdom. She taught us how hard it would be to repent if we made a mistake, and that even if we did repent we could never have the same blessings as before. Of course, by then I had already made my mistakes. Then she made a special point of telling us that only a special few could find the strait and narrow way, and when I looked around that room and saw my competition, all of those goody-goodies, I knew I didn't have a chance of being one of the few. Never kiss boys? Never listen to rock music? Never fight with my mother? Never have an unclean thought? I knew right then I didn't have a snowball's chance, so I just gave up and quit coming."

When I asked her why she had come back to the Church after more than a decade, she answered, "This is where the light is, and I just couldn't stand the dark anymore. At first all I knew was that I had to get out of the dark, but as I moved closer and closer to the light, I finally realized that my teacher hadn't told the truth. There *is* room for me in the kingdom of God, and I don't have to compete with the goody-goodies to get there. I'm not competing with anyone but myself. I have repented; I've already found the strait and narrow way, and as long as I'm just a little better this month than I was last month, just a little nicer, a little kinder, a little more compassionate [or genuinely seek to be (D&C 46:9)]—in his name and for his sake—then I win it all."

INIQUITY

The third hazard in Jesus' warning is the hazard of iniquity: "Because iniquity shall abound, the love of many shall wax cold" (Matthew 24:12). If Satan can't shake us with affliction or trick us with alternate voices and alternate plans, sometimes he'll just try to buy us. In the latter days many will take the money and run—will take the cash, the flesh, or the fame and run from their covenant obligations. A final test of our endurance is *not* falling in love with this world's pleasures. The faithful can't be bought with these things. On Sundays they're in church; they willingly pay tithes and offerings. They keep their physical appetites and desires within bounds, and they are honest in their dealings. Their loyalty is not weakened by the possessions and powers God has placed in their care.

Still, failing to endure is not a sin we commit once for all time. While we remain in mortality, we always have the option of repenting of our failures and trying again. Not long ago, a former student came to see me who had lost his membership as a result of repeated, willful iniquity. He said he wanted to straighten his life out. I asked him if he had a testimony, and he said no, he didn't. Surprised, I asked him why he wanted to repent and regain his membership if he didn't have a testimony. I will never forget his answer: "I don't know that the Church is true, but I know that I once knew, and I know that God knows I once knew. The Church didn't change between then and now—I did. And now I want to know again what I knew before, and I am willing to repent to do it." Even where endurance has failed before the end, repentance can always bring about a new beginning.

Trials, deception, and iniquity—these are the enemies of endurance. Those who can bear the pain of trials, who can ignore the ever-increasing number of alternate voices, who aren't deceived by oxymormons, role-players, or spiritual sadists, those whose loyalty can't be bought with sinful pleasures—these will not betray their Master's trust. They will faithfully maintain the charted course. No matter what happens, their compass-needles always swing back north. They will endure.

Chapter Six

THE PRIME DIRECTIVE

Since this book is about following Christ, some people will be surprised I have not discussed in greater detail specific rules and commandments and how to keep them more exactly. Perhaps that is because I myself quickly feel overwhelmed when I think of the gospel as hundreds of rules, all demanding my immediate attention. I do not deny that the gospel apparently *can* be lived that way by some, but it's too much for me. I am easily daunted by the thought that being right with God consists of mastering many little things and then doing them all in exactly the right way at exactly the right time in exactly the right order.

But on the other hand, perhaps I've left a detailed description of the rules out because some of us too quickly think of enduring to the end in following Christ as a matter of keeping hundreds of rules rather than as a matter of living a few principles. The commandments of God may be expressed either as rules or as principles, depending on the circumstances of those to whom his word is given. Nevertheless, there is a tremendous difference between rules and principles. Rules are usually *based* on principles, but rules are "bite sized," specific applications of principles to certain specified situations. Because of their greater specificity, rules are more rigid and inflexible than principles. By design they offer little choice—other than to obey or disobey—and little wiggleroom. After all, "A rule is a rule." Rules are usually constant; they are the same for every person in every circumstance: "A rule is a rule." And because you don't have to understand a rule in order to obey it, rules are a blessing to the young, the inexperienced, or the spiritually immature.[1] The rules automatically apply higher principles for us to many of life's common situations. This they do in a predetermined and almost mechanical manner that does not require much judgment or discernment on the part of those who keep them: "A rule is a rule." A prime example of righteousness by the rules would be the law of Moses (including the Ten Commandments), which was given to spiritually immature Israel in the wilderness.

Principles, on the other hand, are not rigid and inflexible in how they are observed, and they may often be appropriately adapted and changed to meet special circumstances, though doing this successfully requires more

---

[1] This term is not meant as a put-down for anyone, since everyone is spiritually immature in some area of life.

spiritual maturity and judgment than does merely keeping a rule. That is the great advantage of principle-based righteousness over rule-based righteousness: In order to live our lives by the rules, we would need a rule for every possible human situation, zillions of rules, more than we could ever memorize, but we need only a few principles to live by, and those same few principles can always be appropriately applied to any of life's zillion possible situations. Rules, like the law of Moses, are *fulfilled* (and made obsolete) when we learn and live by the larger principles on which the rules are based. Thus the *principles* of the gospel fulfill the *rules* of the law of Moses, which was a law of "carnal commandments," or a law of rules. For example, in the context of the gospel, the rule against homicide is fulfilled and made obsolete by the principle of love, the rule against adultery by the principle of chastity, and so on. The rules of the law of Moses are good and true, but they are rendered obsolete and unnecessary by living the broader principles of the gospel, which they only partly expressed.

Principle-based living requires a knowledge of the true nature of the God we worship by imitation and of the principles he has revealed in his gospel. We can't live by principles we don't know or follow an example we haven't seen. Principle-based living also requires the gift of the Holy Ghost to guide us as we apply gospel principles to our life situations. Otherwise our carnal minds would influence our interpretation of the principles and subvert our decisions. Finally, principle-based living requires, perhaps most of all, the genuine desire to obey God. Liars who merely want to be freed from the restraint of rules but who do not really want to obey God on a higher level cannot be immediately detected, and they therefore often attempt to use "principle-based living" as an excuse for breaking the rules. Without a genuine desire to obey God, principle-based living quickly becomes an excuse for sin. These are three reasons why true principle-based living can be accomplished only by those who have entered the covenant and keep it. When Joseph Smith was asked how he could govern so many Latter-day Saints, he replied, "I teach them correct principles and they govern themselves." That is, he taught them the principles of the gospel; then the Saints, motivated by a desire to obey God and with the help of the Holy Ghost, decided how to apply those principles to their individual lives. But then they *did* it—they actually followed through and *governed* themselves by the principles of the gospel.[2]

There is much to be said for rule-based righteousness. Many people find it, for a while, the easiest way to make progress toward a Christlike life. It does a good job of teaching us the specifics of what God requires, and it can

---

[2]At BYU one often hears some student who is chafing against the standards say, "Teach us the principles, and then *let* us govern ourselves," a misquoting of the Prophet that really means, "Put the rules in a pamphlet and stop enforcing them." For such as these, rules are a blessing from God. Without all three prerequisites (correct understanding of the principles, the guidance of the Holy Ghost, and the desire to obey) principle-based living will fail.

be an effective training program as we move toward keeping all the commandments all the time (Galatians 3:24). Each of the hundreds of separate elements it keeps in our view are true and important in their own right. And all of us ought to evaluate ourselves from the "rule-based" perspective from time to time just to see how we're doing with all the details and to gauge our progress.

However, I do not personally subscribe to the rule-book approach to living the gospel every day, not because it is bad or wrong, but because there is a *better* way to follow Christ. Not only are broad principles better than the narrow rules they contain; there is also one particular principle that contains within it all the other principles. James calls this principle "the royal law" (James 2:8), and Paul calls it "a more excellent way" (1 Corinthians 12:31). To me it's the difference between trying to keep track of a thousand individual rules, like a thousand little marbles rolling around on a tabletop, and trying to follow one overriding principle, like putting all the marbles into a bag where they can be handled as a single object. In a bag all the marbles are still there, but you only have to keep track of one thing instead of a thousand. In the same way, one principle contains a thousand rules.

The truth is, there is one thing, one single principle, that includes within it *all* the other rules, like marbles in a pouch, so that if we live just that one principle, we automatically live the rules as well. And since there is a limit to the number of pages I can put in this book, and a limit to the number of rules we can be expected to memorize or worry about at one time, it would seem wise and economical, both practically and spiritually, to focus on the one inclusive principle rather than the thousand individual rules. This single principle is the law of love, and if we can get this one principle right, and live it, then we automatically live all of the rules, too. Or at least God will judge it so (1 Peter 4:8; Romans 4:7–8).

That the law of love includes within it all the other laws is made clear by the Apostle Paul: "He that loveth another hath fulfilled the law. For this, Thou shalt not kill, Thou shalt not steal, Thou shalt not bear false witness, Thou shalt not covet; and if there be any other commandment, it is briefly comprehended in this saying, namely, Thou shalt love thy neighbour as thyself. Love worketh no ill to his neighbour: *therefore love is the fulfilling of the law*" (Romans 13:8–10, emphasis added). Now, please don't understand me to be saying anything at all against rule-based righteousness (working from the parts to the whole) or against focusing on a lot of smaller things all at once when you can do it. But if you need a single point to focus on to follow Christ, then this is it.

The Savior himself makes it clear in both the New Testament and the Book of Mormon that there is one thing, one principle, that more than anything else makes us true children of our Father in Heaven: "Love your enemies . . . that ye may be the children of your Father which is in heaven."[3] Do you want to be a true son or

---

[3]Matthew 5:44–45; 3 Nephi 12:44–45.

daughter of God? Then love your enemies (and your friends, too, I would guess), for God loves and blesses all his children. Do you want to be like God? Then cultivate the one trait above all others that characterizes God— love *all* your brothers and sisters as he loves *all* his children.

In the gospel of Jesus Christ, the commandment to love is the Prime Directive, so to speak. It is the first and most important principle in eternity. It is the single most important principle of the gospel and includes all the rules within itself. Loving others and acting accordingly will make us more like God than any other principle. Unfortunately, it also seems to be the element many of us forget first when we start trying to "be religious." Many "religious" people, especially those relying on the rule-based approach, come to think that religion is about what we eat, or how we vote, or how many meetings we attend, or how much money we pay, or how many pages we read. All those things are important, but none of them is *most* important.[4] It is possible to be "active" in church and still be spiritually dead, particularly if we fail to love one another. That is what Paul and Moroni are telling us in 1 Corinthians 13 and Moroni 7:

---

[4]The danger of teaching the law of love is that invariably some spiritually immature persons will pit love against obedience. That will not work. We can *keep* the commandments through principles, like the law of love, or *keep* them through individual rules—but we can't *keep* the command to love God by *breaking* his commandments (John 14:21).

Though I speak with the tongues of men and of angels, and have not charity, I am become as sounding brass, or a tinkling cymbal. And though I have the gift of prophecy, and understand all mysteries, and all knowledge; and though I have all faith, so that I could remove mountains [that is, though I may have all the other attributes of piety], and have not charity, I am nothing. . . . Charity never faileth. . . . And now abideth faith, hope and charity, these three; but the greatest of these is charity.[5]

If a man be meek and lowly in heart, and confesses by the power of the Holy Ghost that Jesus is the Christ, he must needs have charity; for if he have not charity he is nothing; wherefore he must needs have charity. . . . Wherefore, my beloved brethren, if ye have not charity, ye are nothing, for charity never faileth. Wherefore, cleave unto charity, which is the greatest of all.[6]

The Prime Directive has been delivered to us pointedly by the Savior no fewer than three times in John's Gospel alone: "A new commandment I give unto you, That ye love one another; as I have loved you, that ye also love one another. By this shall all men know that ye are my disciples, if ye have love one to another" (John 13:34–35). "This is my commandment, That ye love one another, as I have loved you. Greater love hath no man

---

[5]1 Corinthians 13:1–2, 8, 13.
[6]Moroni 7:44, 46.

than this, that a man lay down his life for his friends" (John 15:12–13). "These things I command you, that ye love one another" (John 15:17).[7]

Matthew records the delivery of the Prime Directive on another occasion. When asked what the most important commandment was, Jesus answered, "Thou shalt love the Lord thy God with all thy heart, and with all thy soul, and with all thy mind. This is the first and great commandment. And the second is like unto it, Thou shalt love thy neighbour as thyself. On these two commandments hang all the law and the prophets" (Matthew 22:37–40).

This is not emotional fluff. This is not pie in the sky, wishful thinking, or idealistic gas. Love is not some subsidiary principle that allows the weepy among us to go off on a crying jag. It's not just something thrown in for the benefit of the sisters or for the super-sensitive "artsy" types. It is not an option that may be ignored by those who would prefer not to clutter their lives with other peoples' problems. There is a grand key here, probably the grandest of them all. It is this: *the heart and soul of the gospel is love, and all the rest is commentary.* Whatever else we may perceive religion to be, we are wrong—for true religion is love in action—God's love for us and our love for God and for our neighbors.

But surely, one may say, if I'm personally righteous, and I've got a Ph.D., and I'm a stake president or a Relief

---

[7]See also 1 John 4:7, 20; 2 John 1:5.

Society president, and I pay 20-percent tithing, and I have fifteen children, and I went on a mission, and I got married in the temple, and I'm an Eagle Scout, and I have *two* years' worth of food storage, and my genealogy is done all the way back to Adam—surely for all this God will exalt me even if I'm not a very compassionate person and don't really love my brothers and sisters.

Wrong!

Listen to Joseph Smith: "To be justified before God we must love one another."[8]

Listen to Nephi: "The Lord God hath given a commandment that all men should have charity, which charity is love. And except they should have charity they were nothing."[9]

Listen to Alma: "If ye do not remember to be charitable, ye are as dross, which the refiners do cast out, (it being of no worth) and is trodden under foot of men."[10]

Listen to Moroni: "This love which thou hast had for the children of men is charity; wherefore, *except men shall have charity they cannot inherit that place which thou hast prepared* in the mansions of thy Father."[11]

Listen to Paul (again): "Though I speak with the tongues of men and of angels, and have not charity, I am

---

[8]*History of the Church* 2:229.

[9]2 Nephi 26:30.

[10]Alma 34:29, where charity equals love and "charitable" equals "motivated by love."

[11]Ether 12:34 (emphasis added). See also Moroni 10:21, where we are also informed we cannot be saved in the kingdom of God without charity (love).

become as sounding brass, or a tinkling cymbal. And though I have the gift of prophecy, and understand all mysteries, and all knowledge; and though I have all faith, so that I could remove mountains, and have not charity, I am nothing."[12]

Listen to Peter: "Seeing ye have purified your souls in obeying the truth through the Spirit unto unfeigned love of the brethren, see that ye love one another with a pure heart fervently."[13]

Listen to John: "Beloved, let us love one another: for love is of God; and every one that loveth is born of God, and knoweth God. He that loveth not knoweth not God; for God is love."[14]

Love is the *sine qua non* of the kingdom of God, the "without-which-not" of celestial glory. Other things may be required as well, but without love in our hearts for God and for our fellow beings, we will not be raised up to a throne. There are no exceptions. We cannot become like God, we cannot be true sons and daughters of God without love—for God *is* love.

STARTING FROM THE WRONG END

Much religious anxiety is created by people starting doctrinally from the wrong end of things, with odds and ends instead of with first principles or with the Prime

---

[12] 1 Corinthians 13:1–2.
[13] 1 Peter 1:22.
[14] 1 John 4:7–8.

Directive. For example, if we start with the doctrine of hell and the suffering promised those who disobey the commandments, it is easy to conclude that God is some kind of cosmic bully with a stick, just itching to smash those who won't do what he says. (I know members of the Church who actually believe this!) But if we start at the right end, with the Prime Directive (God is love, and to become like him we must love), then we more easily see that God is a Father trying to warn precious children where the hidden reefs and hazards are located and guide us home to himself. The sufferings of the disobedient are not the retribution of an offended and vengeful autocrat but the natural consequences of ignored warnings from a loving parent who pleads for us to pay attention. The commandments are not a list of God's arbitrary demands or hoops we have to jump through to please him but a chart through the reefs of life compiled by someone who knows these waters.

Another example of starting from the wrong end can be found in the pain and anxiety of those who agonize over questions of who is sealed to whom. (I'm sealed to A, and I want to be sealed to B; or, Mom and Dad are divorced and sealed to separate partners, so I can't be sealed to the parents I love; and so forth.) Now, I can't answer most of the questions people have on these subjects, but I can help with some of the pain: Start at the right end—start with God's perfect love and his wonderful promises. That great being who is pure love has promised us a fullness of joy if we are true and faithful to our covenants[15]—not just happiness, not just a better life there than here, but a *fullness* of joy, in other words, so much joy we could not possibly under any circumstances have more. So instead of starting with me or Mom being sealed to the wrong person and concluding "therefore I can't possibly be happy in the celestial kingdom," start with the infinite love of God and the promise of a *fullness* of joy and (using a little faith) conclude "therefore this problem is going to be sorted out somehow *to my perfect satisfaction and joy.*" However God works this out—and he's going to do something—it's exactly what we would choose if we only had all the information and all the powers that God has. We are going to be absolutely, fully, and completely satisfied. We have to be, or our joy isn't *full* as we've been promised. No one in the celestial kingdom will be sealed to someone he or she doesn't want to be with—that wouldn't be a *fullness* of joy. No one will lose a loved one he or she can't be sealed to—that wouldn't be a *fullness* of joy either.[16] I don't know how God will sort these things out, but I know that he loves us; I know he's promised that the faithful will receive "all things"; I know he's promised them a fullness of joy—and I believe him on all

---

[15]See John 15:11; 16:24; 2 Nephi 9:18; D&C 101:36; 138:17 among others. The words of Christ to the Three Nephites are pertinent to all who will receive of his fullness (see 3 Nephi 28:10).

[16]See Elder Boyd K. Packer's conference address in April of 1994 and his wonderful assurance that faithful parents will not "lose" their less-faithful children. If God has promised me all things, how can that not somehow include my babies?

counts.[17] "Eye hath not seen, nor ear heard, neither have entered into the heart of man, the things which God hath prepared for them that love him" (1 Corinthians 2:9). In other words, we can't even imagine how great this is going to be! So stop worrying or complaining in advance, and trust him—you're going to *love* this.[18]

GOD'S WORK

Sometimes, by starting from the wrong end, we forget that God's business isn't damnation but *salvation*. I don't recall ever seeing God described in scripture as "the Terminator," but I do recall seeing the term "Savior" a couple of times. I don't recall those who attempt to imitate Christ and do his work ever being called "Destroyers on Mt. Zion" or "Punishers on Mt. Zion." No, we are to be, like him, "Saviors"—"Saviors on Mt. Zion." So what is God all about? (We'd better know if we're trying to be like him.) According to John, "God is love." And how exactly is this love expressed? What does God *do?* He tells us himself in the Pearl of Great Price: "This is my work and my glory, to bring to pass the immortality and eternal life of man" (Moses 1:39). God's work is *us!* What

---

[17]Think about it. God says he will give the faithful "all things." What isn't included in "all things?" What will I *not* have if God gives me "all things"? The magnitude of that promise boggles my mind and solves all my problems. All I have to do is endure faithfully.

[18]Understand, of course, that those who complain the loudest about the shortcomings of the gospel plan are usually not those who try to live it. In their case the complaints are moot, for the fullness comes only to the faithful.

he does for a living is to make us wretched humans be more, be better, be greater.

It is vital we understand that this scripture doesn't apply only to God's celestial children but to *all* of them. The many mansions in our Father's house include the terrestrial and telestial kingdoms as well as the celestial. They are all kingdoms of *glory*. It isn't just his obedient children who are part of God's work and glory and for whom he labors; it is all of them who will be redeemed from the devil and raised to any degree of glory whatever (see, for example, D&C 76:42–43, 85, 88–89). In other words, God improves *everybody*; he blesses everyone and everything he touches; it is his nature to raise and to bless. He has raised us from whatever we were before we were spirits to make us his spirit children. He has given those of his children who would allow it physical bodies. And in the resurrection he will give us eternal glory to the degree that we have allowed it. God tries to give all his children celestial glory, but if we resist that, he tries to give us terrestrial glory. And if we resist that, he tries to give us telestial glory. It is his work to maximize our eternal condition, to get us the best deal in eternity that he can—it's what he does for a living. Naturally, he wants to give us all everything, but of course most of us resist him—so he gives us what he can. It's his job—his "work"; and it's what makes him great—his "glory." Saving us and improving us is what he's all about.

Now, if we are going to inherit his kingdom, we must imitate God and become like him. That means we also—

like him—must love all God's children and improve everyone and everything we touch. If our children or our friends resist our attempts to help them gain celestial glory, we must then fall back and do what we can to help them gain terrestrial glory. And if they resist that, we must work to get them into the penthouse, rather than the basement, of the telestial glory. But if we are to be like God and to become gods, then we, like him, must to the extent that we are able bless and raise and improve all with whom we come in contact—not just our obedient children and not just our neighbors who might join the Church.

Several years ago I delivered a Know-Your-Religion lecture in which the topic of God's love came up. After the lecture, a woman approached me and said, "Brother Robinson, I'd like your opinion on something. My husband and I have told our daughter all her life that if she would get married in the temple we would pay for everything, but if she didn't get married in the temple, she was on her own, and neither she nor her husband would be welcome in our home. Well, do you know what she's done? She's gotten pregnant and can't get married in the temple! So we're going to keep our word. We won't be attending the wedding, and until she straightens out her life, we don't want anything to do with her. Some of our friends think we are being a little too harsh, but she knew what she was doing, and it's on her own head. What do you think?"

What I dearly wanted to say, but didn't, was this: "I

think that for the next couple of years when you attend church you and your husband ought to try *standing* on the pews instead of sitting in them. That way, possibly, the things being taught there won't continue going over your head."

What I did say was this: "Look, those of us who are in the gospel covenant are not in the condemnation business—that's Satan's self-appointed role. We're in the *salvation* business here. OK, your daughter isn't living the celestial law right now, but how close can you keep her to it? She isn't going to be married in the temple, but will she get married in the Church and let the bishop perform the ceremony instead of going to Las Vegas or something? Will she feel good about the Church and feel loved by her friends and family there? Will her positive experiences with the Church lead her in the future to welcome home teachers and visiting teachers into her home, people who may in time help this young couple be active in the Church and eventually be sealed in the temple? What can be *salvaged* here, Sister, and how can it be done? Do God's work—*improve* your daughter and help her rise as far as she can. God's work and glory has as much to do with helping some of his beloved children find telestial and terrestrial glory as it does helping a smaller number find celestial glory. So be like God, bring your daughter as close as you can, lift her and love her as much as you can—as much as she will allow. If I were you, I'd go home right now and call your daughter. Apologize to her and ask her how you and your husband can help her out in her new circumstances. Then go buy a swing and a car seat for the baby and hope your daughter forgives you."

Do you have troubled or unfaithful children? Then picture the following scene. I can't prove it represents true doctrine, but I dearly believe it does. Suppose the Father brings you a little baby spirit and says, "This child is going to have more problems than most in mortality, but I know that if she is raised in your home she will rise higher and go farther than if she were anywhere else. Will you take her and love her and maximize her potential? It will be hard, because she's not going to get straight A's, and she won't win any awards. There will be things she can't overcome, and there will at times be great pain for you. But she is my baby, and she is precious to me, and I know she will go farther and rise higher with you for her parents than with anyone else. Won't you please take her and love her as I do?"

I believe that many righteous parents with troubled children volunteered in a premortal life to take those children to help them reach a higher state of glory than they could otherwise have received. Not even God can exalt all his children. We must remember that our task is not necessarily to exalt all of ours but to imitate God in lifting and blessing all our children (and his) as much as they will allow us to—even the ones who are troubled. And in the resurrection, when they have learned better and have finally turned again to God, they will say, "All that I have gained I owe to my Savior and to my noble parents." And they will rise up and thank and bless us for our love and patience and sacrifices in their behalf.[19]

UNCONDITIONAL LOVE?

There has been a great deal of discussion about God's "unconditional" love lately, and most of the discussion has not been very useful. If God is love, and if the Prime Directive is to love as God loves, then is God's love "unconditional," and should mine also be "unconditional"? That is a loaded question, for *unconditional* means different things to different people, and the core of the misunderstanding lies in those different definitions. (Note that "unconditional love" is not a scriptural term, and I think it is not a very useful one. It has been my experience that whenever people discuss the scriptures using nonscriptural terms, they usually get into trouble, like the Nicene fathers did with *trinity* or *homoousios*.)[20]

For some people, God's "unconditional" love means that God will accept everyone on equal terms, no matter what they may have done in life. He won't hold our sins against us, and ultimately he will forgive everyone everything and deny no one any of the blessings given to anyone else. "The righteous have no advantage and the wicked no disadvantage," they would argue, "because

---

[19]Again, this is only my opinion—and my hope—but I do believe it to be so.

[20]*Homoousios* is an unscriptural Greek word meaning "of the same essence." It was used in the Nicene Creed to describe the relationship of the Father and Son.

these are conditions, and God's love and approval are 'unconditional.'" That, of course, is totally false. Many of our Father's children will never even see him again, for they will not be allowed into his presence in their filthy state, except perhaps for judgment.

However, in denying that God's love is "unconditional" in that sense, it is possible to go too far and deny that he loves his children at all, insisting rather that he loves only his "good" children—and even them only *after* they've repented and entered into the gospel covenant. That is also false. The same divine love that causes the heavens to rejoice over the repentant and righteous causes them to weep over the rebellious and wicked (Moses 7:28, 37). Good or bad, we are his children, and in either case God loves us—he loves *all* of us.

Those who speak against God's loving all his children usually start with a scripture like John 15:10, "If ye keep my commandments, ye shall abide in my love," which clearly states a condition for "abiding in his love." The doctrinal misunderstanding arises from equating "being loved by God" with "abiding in God's love," for those two phrases do not describe the same state. God can love us whether we return his love or not. His loving us does not require our emotional response. But for us to "abide in his love" requires our willingness so to abide. God can love me without my consent, but he can't have a relationship with me—I don't "*abide* in his love"—unless *I* agree to it. Love defined as the desire to have a relationship can be unilateral—it requires (alas) only one party.

But love *as* a relationship requires two parties. I can be "in love" with a woman who does not love me back (and I have been). It is painful, one-sided—and unconditional. It's just there. But no matter how much I may love that person, we do not have a relationship. Though *I* may be in love, *we* are not—because the relationship isn't there, only my desire for it. She cannot "abide in my love," even though I may want her to, because she refuses to do so.

Similarly God's love (understood as his desire for a relationship with us) is unconditional. In fact, God commands all men and women everywhere to repent and come to him (3 Nephi 11:32). He desires to redeem us, to glorify and exalt us equally and unconditionally. Does God desire to have an eternal relationship with all his children? Yes, and in this sense God's love is unconditional. "All are invited, none is excluded." But it takes two people to have a relationship. A relationship, by definition, requires *two* points of reference, and only some of God's children love him back and agree to enter into the desired relationship. He does not initially love them any more than the others, but in time the relationship of love that is possible with them is much, much greater than it is with those who reject him. They "abide in his love."

Many of God's children will not love him. They will not accept the proposal of the Bridegroom, though he loves them dearly. They will never experience the joys the gospel marriage brings. However, that is not because God is unwilling or because they failed to meet conditions that would have rendered him willing. It is because they will not accept his proposal; they will not come to the wedding. Though he loved them first, they did not love him back, and by their choice the relationship will not be as great as it might have been—they refuse to "abide in his love."

To summarize, God's love (understood as his desire *for* us) is unconditional. God's love (understood as his relationship *with* us) is conditioned upon our positive response to his wooing of us. The only variable is *us.* Not even God can force another person to love him, and not even God can have the same relationship with those who hate him that he can with those who love him. While God's love might be unconditional, to "abide" in a relationship with him requires *our* participation and *our* love in return.

FAITH, HOPE, AND CHARITY

Most members of the Church understand that faith, hope, and charity (love) are linked together, but perhaps not as many would realize exactly how often they are linked together in scripture or understand why.[21] As we have true faith in Christ, when we begin to believe his good news as well as to believe in him, it finally dawns on us that if Christ can do what he says he can do, then he really *can* save us. There is hope for us. Therefore, if I

---

[21]Romans 5:2–5; 1 Corinthians 13:13; 1 Thessalonians 1:3, 5:8; 1 Peter 1:21–22; 2 Nephi 31:20 (where faith equates with steadfastness); Alma 7:24, 13:29; Ether 12:4, 28; Moroni 7:1, 40–45, 8:14, 10:20; D&C 4:5, 6:19, 12:8, 18:19.

truly believe Christ, then of necessity I must also have hope in my own salvation and exaltation. That is what the book *Believing Christ* was all about. But beyond that, hope in Christ in turn leads to charity (love), and that is what this book is all about. For the expectation of being *with* Christ is also the expectation of being *like* Christ. We cannot come to Christ and worship Christ without becoming what he is—and Christ is love. Therefore of necessity, believing Christ gives us hope of being with Christ, and our anticipation of being with him leads us to imitate him now and to share with others what he has shared with us. True faith in Christ is, in a way, like a disease: it is highly communicable, and it causes us eventually to break out in a rash of hope and love. According to the scriptures, that is how to tell whether someone has faith or not. If people have faith, it will give them hope and move them to love their brothers and sisters (John 13:35).

I have on rare occasions felt the pure love of God pour into my soul. But more often the love of God has come to me mediated through the love of others. I first learned about the love of God through the selflessness of family, friends, and teachers who loved me, made sacrifices for me, and ministered to me in his name. Their names are legion, but I would like to share my experiences with just three. These people who have had such an impact on my life were just ordinary, faithful members of my ward and my family doing their best to live the gospel. I doubt they would have considered themselves the heroes that they are to me.

A PRIMARY TEACHER

When I was ten or eleven years old—a Blazer, I think—my teacher was a sister named Maudie Barron. I cannot remember anything she ever taught me, anything at all. Nor can I remember anything in particular she did that other teachers didn't. But I knew then and know now, although I don't remember her ever saying it, that Sister Barron loved me. I know because I felt it heart to heart. Actually, I do remember one time when another leader was pressuring me to sing a solo part in a song she had arranged for the Primary Christmas program. I'm sure it was important to her that her program be successful, and for some reason, she thought that required my singing this part. I'm also sure she didn't realize how traumatized I was at being forced to sing in front of the other kids, who were teasing and laughing at me. I would have eaten spiders before singing that solo. But this sister just kept playing my part over and over again on the piano, frustrated that I wouldn't sing it, while I stared at the floor in humiliation refusing to sing, speak, or move. Finally, just seconds short of total meltdown, Sister Barron saw my situation, came to the stand, and escorted me from the room. Outside the chapel as I burst into tears, she hugged me and promised me I wouldn't have to sing if I didn't want to. And I knew that she loved me more than she loved the darn program.

Sister Barron had a bad heart, they tell me, but I have never believed it. To this day, almost forty years later, I cannot speak her name without tears coming to my eyes, so great was her impact on me, not just from this one episode but also from many months of kindness, patience, and caring when I was a difficult child at a difficult age. I know that nothing was wrong with her heart, and she is not merely remembered, she is revered. My point is this: Maudie Barron brought me closer to the kingdom of God by her Christlike influence and by flooding me with her genuine love than many other teachers have done with their lessons and activities. I know those lessons helped me a great deal, and I am grateful to those teachers who sacrificed to prepare them. But in the long run the best lesson and the one with the greatest impact on me overall was a Christlike life and an unfeigned love. Even at that young age, I knew that Sister Barron was a lot like our Heavenly Father, and I knew that in eternity I wanted to live in a place where the people were just like her.

Perhaps it's also worth noting, though it grieves me to say it, that Maudie never knew how I felt. By the time I was old enough to tell her, her very excellent heart had stopped working, and she was gone. We don't have to save the world to obey the Prime Directive and be our Heavenly Father's children; we just have to do our part and love each other. And we may never know in this life whom we have touched, blessed, or even saved.

A SCOUTMASTER

Cy Watson was my Scoutmaster for several years and one of the greatest influences for good in my life. Cy was my kind of guy—a grumpy old man. But somehow through the grumpy, we Scouts knew he loved us. Cy sacrificed hours, evenings, and weekends in our behalf. He never missed troop meetings, activities, or courts of honor. He never said he loved us (Cy wouldn't have), but we knew it anyway. And because he loved us, we were willing to be taught by him. Cy taught me how to fold a flag and how to love my country. He taught me that hard work pays off. He taught me to measure twice and cut once. He taught me to close gates and to hate litter. He once made me stand for half an hour "holding up a tree" because I disobeyed the rules. I don't remember what I'd done, but he taught me the law of justice, and that no one was above the law. I learned from Cy, by example, the old-fashioned virtues. I learned that honor was better than wealth and that duty was more pressing than desire or even than need. I didn't learn these things because Cy *told* me, I learned them because Cy *taught* me—because he believed them himself. He believed in the Scout Oath and the Scout Law, and he infused in me his noble values. May God bless him!

Looking back now, I really don't know much about Cy. I know that he contributed in a major way to my present character. I know I respected him. I know I loved him. Cy had a testimony, but he was not ostentatious in things religious. Still, he obeyed the Prime Directive, and the fruit it bore in our ward was a whole generation of boys who became men—not just grownups, but men. I eagerly look forward to seeing him again in the kingdom of God.

GRANDMA LOVED THE BACKS

I did not know my grandmother as well as I could have wished. She lived with relatives in Arizona, and I only saw her once or twice a year. She died while I was still a teenager, but I do remember that Grandma loved the backs. Whenever we had chicken, she would say, "Oh, may I please have the back? I love the backs." That never quite made sense to me. How could anyone actually *love* the backs? I mean, a back was just fried skin on bone with a tiny dab of meat. As a growing boy, I certainly had no such foolish preferences, and I was grateful that my siblings and I got the breasts, the legs, the thighs—got them in part because Grandma preferred the backs. My father tells me that she was always like that. When he was a boy and times were hard on the dry farm, chickens were scarce, and there was seldom more than just enough for such a large family, but even then Grandma loved the backs.

I never figured it out until years later, never even had a clue until I was an adult with my own children, children I loved, children whose happiness was more important to me than my own. One day as my heart swelled with love for my own dear ones, I realized that all her life Grandma had taken the least part for herself and given the best away. It wasn't the backs that Grandma had loved at all; it was her children and grandchildren, her neighbors, her fellowman—and her Savior. Oh, Grandma, thank you for the lesson. I'll try harder to love the backs.

PASS IT ON

The ultimate expression of following Christ is to receive his love, whether from himself or from those who serve him, to be lifted and blessed by it and then to be for others what he has been for us—lifting and blessing them with our love in turn. Someone out there will experience the love of God first and foremost through you. The love of God radiates outward like ripples from a stone thrown in a pond, like an infection that spreads from person to person. The royal law is "As I have loved you, love one another." Then pass it on! We cannot always pay back the same individuals who have loved and served us most. Grandma and Maudie Barron and Cy Watson are all gone. By the time I realized how much I owed them, I could no longer pay *them* back. Then what must I do to clear the debt? I must pass it on; I must be for someone else what these Saints have been for me.

I repay my parents and grandparents for their love by loving my children and grandchildren—who will in turn love and bless their children and grandchildren. I repay my teachers for their love by teaching others and loving those I teach. And they in turn will love and teach still others so that my influence, which is Cy's influence,

Maudie's influence, Grandma's influence—and ultimately the Savior's influence—will never end. As Christ loved and served those who could never repay him, so I must love and serve those who will never repay me, and they in turn will love and serve still others who can never repay them. In that way, love truly never ends (1 Corinthians 13:8); it ripples outward forever and ever. In becoming part of that chain, we become part of an eternity of love in which the Father and the Son are also links. And in this we truly follow Christ.

We can love Christ, too, but we can't really do much for him personally. I mean, he pretty much has everything he needs by now. (It's that age-old problem: "What can you get for the man who has everything?") Well, we sure can't save him. We can't bind up his wounds, carry his burdens, or lessen his pain. We can't feed him when he's hungry or clothe him or take care of him when he's sick—for he is far beyond all that now. So how, then, shall we appropriately express our love for him? He has told us how in Matthew 25:34–40:

> Then shall the King say unto them on his right hand, Come, ye blessed of my Father, inherit the kingdom prepared for you from the foundation of the world: For I was an hungered, and ye gave me meat: I was thirsty, and ye gave me drink: I was a stranger, and ye took me in: Naked, and ye clothed me: I was sick, and ye visited me: I was in prison, and ye came unto me.
>
> Then shall the righteous answer him, saying,

> Lord, when saw we thee an hungered, and fed
> thee? or thirsty, and gave thee drink? When saw
> we thee a stranger, and took thee in? or naked,
> and clothed thee? Or when saw we thee sick, or
> in prison, and came unto thee?
>
> And the King shall answer and say unto
> them, Verily I say unto you, Inasmuch as ye
> have done it unto one of the least of these my
> brethren, ye have done it unto me.

Christ invites us to repay our debt to him by blessing
others in turn. Our neighbors in their need become sym-
bolic of Christ, and in filling their needs as he has filled
ours, we partially pay our debt to him. Also, as we minister to those who need our help, we adopt *his* role as the
one who blesses. Thus, as we minister to them, we follow him; as we minister to them, we *become* him. Those
we serve take on our former role as recipients of his love
and grace, and by serving them we "move up" and take
on *his* role as the one who loves, blesses, and saves. We
become saviors on Mt. Zion for those we serve; we are
exalted—raised up to his level and to his function—by
our love and service to others.[22]

Now go out and find him. Find him and minister to
him. Find him in the faces of your family, friends, neighbors, students, colleagues, and strangers on the street.
Search him out. Dress his wounds. Feed him. Clothe

---

[22]I understand that being "saviors on Mt. Zion" is associated primarily with work for the dead. I merely suggest that it could refer to
saving work for the *living* as well—our everyday work at our everyday
callings in our everyday families, wards, and branches.

him. Serve him. Teach him. Love him. For this is the Prime Directive, the "royal law," the "more excellent way." In this way more than in any other, we truly follow him.

INDEX

Accountability, personal, 113
Accusations of Satan, 114–16
Activity, church, 25–26
Adam and Eve, 46, 48–49
Adoption, example of, 13–14
Afflictions: degree of
    difficulty counts in, 35–37;
    enduring, 91–92; examples
    of, 93–95
Agency, 16–17
Aging, 50–51
Antinomianism, 89
Apostasy, 120
Atonement, 49, 59
Awareness, personal, 25–26

Baptism: essential for
    salvation, 1–2, 4; as our
    part of the covenant, 6; and
    membership in the
    kingdom of God, 7–8,
    17–18; and enduring to the
    end, 25
Barron, Maudie, 152–53

Behavior, 72, 76, 81
Believing: essential for
    salvation, 1–2, 4; as our
    part of the covenant, 6; and
    membership in the
    kingdom of God, 7–8,
    17–18; and enduring to the
    end, 25; faith as, 83–84. *See
    also* Faith
Benson family rumors, 107
Benson, Reed, 107
Blessings, 36–37
Brown, Willmia, 104

Carnal self: turning from,
    40–42, 63; serves devil,
    57–58, 117–19; influence
    of, diminishes, 61–62; sees
    sin as desirable, 88
Change, the mighty, 40–42,
    62
Charity, 136–39
Chicken backs, example of,
    155–56

Choices: if no, then no
condemnation, 37; reveal
true character, 47; in
mortality, 60–61
Chores, spiritual, 75–76
Church of Jesus Christ:
joining, as entering the
covenant, 6–7; members of,
are already in kingdom of
God, 7–8, 13, 15, 17, 22–23;
likened to bride, 15–16;
members of, have agency,
16–17; members of, must
endure to the end within,
29–30; is true, 110; false
accusations against,
115–20. *See also* Latter-day
Saints
Commandments: keeping,
and being "in Christ,"
77–78; to avoid deception,
99; as rules or principles,
129–30; greatest, 133–37
Commitment, inner, 24–28
Common sense, 53
Condemnation as Satan's
business, 145
Condescension of God, 68
Conscience, 56
Consequences, natural, 140
Conversion: temptations
come even after, 41–42;
Church members must
move beyond, 69–70;
precedes good works, 73–74
Couch potatoes, spiritual, 74
Countenance, change of, 72
Covenant, gospel: entering, as
becoming one with Christ,

2, 4; conditions of, 6;
Church members have
already entered, 7–8, 12–13,
15, 17–18,; analogous to
marriage, 15–16; God is
bound to, 16–17; renewing,
31–32, 39; as gift of grace,
80–81; faithfulness to, 83;
entering, as two-part
relationship, 149–50

Death, 50–51
Deception: as hazard to
endurance, 97–98: under
guise of revelation, 99–104;
found in rumors, 104–8;
from false prophets,
108–11; lies as, 112–16;
from internal carnal self,
116–20; hypocrisy as,
120–24; from spiritual
masochists and sadists,
124–26
Degree of difficulty analogy,
35–37
Determination, personal,
25–26
Disposition, change in, 41–42
Divers, parable of, 34–37

Elevator rumor, 106
Emotions in fallen state,
55–56
Enduring to the end:
definition of, 18, 21–25,
65–66; commitment to,
26–28; other components
of, 29–30; as not rejecting
Savior, 37–38; as staying on

train, 68; as our choice, 81;
as faithfulness to the end,
92–94; failure at, can be
repented of, 127
Eternal life. See Kingdom of
God.
Extra credit in kingdom of
heaven, 35–37

Faith: accepting life's test
because of, 59; James'
definition of, versus Paul's,
83–84; lack of, by spiritual
masochists, 124; motivates
to love, 151. See also
Believing
Faithfulness: as being trusted,
23–24; as part of enduring
to the end, 25; as spiritual
knowledge, 27; renewing,
32–34; as intended by Paul,
83–84
Fall, the: understanding, 44–
45; planned by God, 47–49;
physical effects of, 50–51;
spiritual effects of, 51–52;
mental effects of, 52–55;
emotional effects of, 55–56;
moral effects of, 56–57;
accepting, through trust in
Christ, 59–60; all effects of,
overcome by Savior, 61, 63
Fanatics, 111
Fear and trembling, 87–88
Fishing, example of, 12
Flesh and service to devil,
56–57

Gate to kingdom of heaven, 8,
17, 22–23, 71
Glory, kingdoms of, 143
God: covenants with us, 6;
Church members already
in family of, 14; knowing
nature of, 131, 140;
business of, to improve
everyone, 143; loves us
unconditionally, 147–50.
See also Jesus Christ,
Kingdom of God
Godhood, Saints to try,
144–46. See also Imitation
Goose-pimple gang, 105–8
Gospel of Jesus Christ: as
correct yardstick, 54–55;
those who try to improve,
are deceived, 112; as love,
136–39. See also Church of
Jesus Christ
Grace, 78–80, 90

Handicaps: physical, 50–51;
spiritual, 51–52; mental,
52–55; emotional, 55–56;
moral, 56–57; mortal, 66
Happiness, 74
Holy Ghost, receiving:
essential for salvation, 4;
sanctifies, 5; as God's
confirmation of covenant,
6; and membership in
kingdom of God, 7–8,
17–18; as part of enduring
to the end, 25; need for, 56,
131
Humility, 85–86
Hypocrisy: Saints unjustly

accused of, 118–19; types
of, 120–24

Imitation: of Christ, 70,
158–59; of God, 143–46,
150–51
Ingratitude, 87
Iniquity as hazard for
endurance, 126–27
Integrity, 23
Intellect, flawed, 52–55
Intellectuals, 108, 114

James and faith, 79, 83
Jesus Christ: becoming one
with, 4–5; as bridegroom,
15–16; following, from
within kingdom, 18;
remaining faithful to, 29,
37–38; putting trust in
atonement of, 59–60; goal
to be like, 67–68; coming
unto, 69–70; imitating, 70,
158–59; as Savior, 80–81;
showing love for, 157–58
Joy, 74, 141
Justification, 4–5

Kingdom of God: inheriting,
1, 31–33; Church members
already in, 7–8, 16–17–18,
65, 71; dual meanings of,
9–11; on earth, is in
Church of Jesus Christ, 30;
doing works to build, 73
Kingdom of heaven, 9–10

Labor and happiness, 74
Latter-day Saints: and term

saved, 3, 11; meaning of,
5–6; seek to imitate Christ,
67–68, 156–57; seek
godhood, 68–70, 144–46; as
stones, 72–73; deception of,
103–4; as "suckers," 104–8;
as saviors on Mt. Zion,
158–59
Law of Moses, 130–31
Legends, urban, 108
Lies, 112–14
Light of Christ, 56
Love: as motivator, 88–89;
law of, as ultimate
principle, 133–35; as heart
and soul of gospel, 136–39;
brings fullness of joy,
140–41; as God loves,
142–46; God's
unconditional, 147–50;
examples of Christlike,
152–56; passing, on, 156–57
Loyalty. See Faithfulness

Marriage, analogies of, 15–16,
23, 28, 31, 96–97
Masochists, spiritual, 124
Media, 114
Mercy, 87–88
Missionaries arguing faith
versus works, 79–80
Moral reasoning, flawed,
56–57
"More or less" principle,
110–12
Mortality, 45–47
Mysteries, 101–2

Naval ship example, 40

Nephite on the Mesa rumor, 107

"No-win" situation, 45

Obedience, 75, 82, 135

Offenses as modern afflictions, 96–97

Opposition, internal, 116–17

Oxymormons, 120–21

Page, Hiram, 102

Parable: of the talents, 34; of the divers, 34–37

Patriarchal blessings, 107–8

Paul and faith, 79, 83

Perfection, 31–32, 39, 63

Physical stamina, 22–23

Pioneers, 92

Politics, 108–9

Pre-existence, 46–47

Priesthood, 103, 106

Prime Directive, 135–37. *See also* Love

Principles, living by, 131–32

Priorities, 109

Promises, keeping. *See* Enduring to the end

Prophets: true, 100–102; false, 108, 111–12

Reason, flawed, 52–55

Rebellion, 116–17

Relationship of father and child, 75. *See also* Covenant, gospel

Reliability, 22

Religion, incorrect uses of, 104–5

Repentance: essential for salvation, 1–2, 4; as our part of the covenant, 6–7, 31, 59–60; and membership in the kingdom of God, 7–8, 17–18; ongoing, necessary, 24, 38–40; as part of enduring to the end, 25; available to all, 124–25; brings new beginning, 127

Resentment, 117–18

Resistance to carnality, 62–63

Resurrection, 55–56, 61

Revelation, personal, 101–3, 107–8, 111

Righteousness, 41, 88–89

Rogers, Aurelia Spencer, 95

Role-players, 121–24

Rules, 129–30, 132–33

Rumors: Saints' gullibility toward, 104–5; of prophet in the elevator, 106; of Nephite on the Mesa, 107; of Benson Family special revelations, 107; from patriarchal blessings and missionary stories, 108

Sacrament, 24, 31–32, 39, 66

Sadists, spiritual, 125–26

Safety within kingdom of God, 18, 21

Salvation: conditional, 3; as present reality, 11; as process, 66–67, 70–71; only through the Savior, 70, 81; and good works, 76–78; understanding of "working out own," 85–86; do-it-yourself, pits faith

against works, 89; God's business as, 142–43; mortals in business of, 145
Sanctification, 4–5
Satan: as abuser, 91–92; as deceiver, 98–99; snares of, 103–4; loves fanatics and rebels, 111; as liar, 112–13; as accuser, 114–16
Saved, being, 2–3, 11–12, 69
Savior on Mt. Zion, 158. See also Jesus Christ
Sealings, 140–41
Second-string performance, 32–34
Self-indulgence, 124
Separation anxiety, 51
Servants, 82
Service to Christ, 81
Sin, personal: repentance of, 30–31; as effect of the Fall, 58; choosing, 60–61; as its own punishment, 88–89
Slavery, 81–82
Snares of Satan, 103–4
Soccer team, analogy of, 32–34
Sower, parable of, 28–29
Spencer, Howard Orson, 95
Spencer, Orson, 94–95
Spirit, discernment of, 57
Spiritual masochists and sadists, 62, 124–26
Spiritual trauma, 52
Stewardship, 101–2
Stones, analogy of, 72–73
Suffering, 22
Swim meet analogy, 34–37

Tabloid religion, 105
Talents, 32–34
Temisevä, Helvi, 93–94
Temptations, 41–42
Test in mortality, 47–48, 58–59, 61
Testify, working to, 72
Testimony, 27–28
Train analogy, 67–69
Transgression, 49
Trials, 35–37
Trust, 23
Truth and Satan's lies, 112–13

Unfaithfulness, 33–34, 120–21
Universe, 112

Voices, alternative, 108–13

Watson, Cy, 154–55
Wolves in sheeps' clothing, 108
Word of Wisdom, 111
Work of kingdom: as process for salvation, 66–70; as worship, 71–72; to testify, 72; to build kingdom, 73–74; necessary for God's children, 75
Works: as part of relationship, 75–76; and salvation, 76–78; and grace, 78–79; as token of righteousness, 81; necessary for salvation, 90; as confirmation of our loyalty, 82
Worship, 71–72
Wrong end, starting at, 139–41